STRATEGIC IT ACCESSIBILITY: ENABLING THE ORGANIZATION

2nd Edition

Jeff Kline

To family, friends, peers and everyone out there
trying to make the digital world inclusive.

CONTENTS

Introduction ix

CHAPTER 1. An Overview of IT Accessibility 1

CHAPTER 2. IT Accessibility Technical Enablement versus Business Transformation 13

CHAPTER 3. The Case for Accessibility 19

CHAPTER 4. Getting Started 37

CHAPTER 5. Organizing IT Accessibility 51

CHAPTER 6. Cost and Funding Models for the IT Accessibility Initiative 67

CHAPTER 7. The Stakeholder Organizations: Where IT Accessibility Plays 77

CHAPTER 8. The Focus Areas 93

CHAPTER 9. Putting It All Together 169

CHAPTER 10. Workplace Management for Employees with Disabilities 179

CHAPTER 11. Maintaining Momentum 187

CASE STUDY ING Netherlands Strategic Accessibility 195

Reference Information 203

Glossary 206

About the Author 221

INTRODUCTION

If you are reading this book, odds are you already know that access to information technology (IT) for people with disabilities is a complex topic. Whether your organization is in the public or the private sector, IT accessibility can affect it in profound ways. Making IT accessible enables people with disabilities all over the world to gain access to the information, experiences, and opportunities that other users enjoy and even take for granted. IT accessibility truly touches the lives of people with disabilities in wonderful ways.

IT accessibility is most familiar in the context of products or communications or information aimed at the consumer, such as websites. Within these areas, most organizations are aware that laws require them to become more accessible to those with special needs. Organizations may even have the technical knowledge needed to do so. However, addressing every aspect of IT accessibility, both legally and from the perspective of the user, is more complicated than it first appears. Becoming completely IT accessible requires vision, thoughtfulness, and action in key areas of your organization and the IT you sell or use. For example, a company may need to consider the ramifications of IT accessibility in software architecture and technology selection, education and training, or development and test environments. While making an organization's IT accessible certainly involves technical challenges, technical execution is the tactical piece within the ecosystem of accessibility.

Asking questions at the beginning of a project—"Does this product or service need to be accessible? If so, how can my organization accomplish this?"—is part of the first step. The answers to these questions may be relatively easy or quite difficult, especially the first time, depending on several factors.

If it hasn't already, at some point, your organization will determine that IT accessibility is more than an option: it is a key to success. Questions about IT accessibility will begin to move away from the tactical and gravitate toward understanding and addressing the strategic aspects of IT accessibility: "How can we ensure that the next product or service we offer—and the three after that, and the new website—will be accessible to people with disabilities, even through the inevitable internal organizational changes, personnel turnover, new technical challenges, or other events that can affect accessibility?"

1.1 TAKING STOCK

Taken a step further, after factoring in your organization's worldwide internal IT environment, a new and far-reaching question will emerge: "Is our application environment and infrastructure accessible to the people with disabilities on our staff and in all stages of our employees' lives? Are we staffing (externally or internally), gainfully employing, and technically supporting people with disabilities, preventing their exclusion from the workplace, and avoiding litigation?"

Even when companies try to make their products and services accessible to satisfy regulatory or customer-accessibility requirements, they often neglect IT access internally, forgetting about their own employees with disabilities. The shoemaker's children need shoes too.

When thinking about diversity, it's important to realize that your employees with disabilities are unlike other diversity groups, such as women, African Americans, Hispanics, and on. Protecting these groups from discrimination in hiring and promoting, and from workplace harassment, can generally be accomplished through good human-relations policy and resource management. When discrimination occurs, it's typically a human-based problem, such as a manager who chooses not to hire someone from a minority group because the manager doesn't think the candidate will "fit well" with the "regular folks" on staff, or because the manager is ignorant or just plain racist or sexist. Such problems are typically managed in a human-based fashion, one would hope within the organization but perhaps in the courtroom.

While human-based issues can certainly arise concerning employees with disabilities, one fundamental aspect separates them from all the other diversity groups: *they are highly dependent on IT accessibility in the workplace to perform their work at any useful level.*

Also important to bear in mind is that the word "disabled" applies to a varied group, including those with disabilities involving sight, hearing, mobility, and cognitive impairments, as well as people with a temporary disability (as a result of injury, for example.) Also, it's important to note that there are other groups not traditionally identified as people with disabilities but who experience challenges similar to those identified as having disabilities. The aging population is an example of such a group.

Has your organization thought in depth about IT accessibility? How many applications or web pages does your organization provide every day that employees use in their work? If the answer is "a lot," then making all of your internal IT accessible may seem daunting. In many cases, providing internal IT accessibility may be more challenging than providing IT accessibility for outside users.

1.2 ACHIEVING IT ACCESSIBILITY

Now that you understand the need for IT accessibility, both within the company itself and in the products and services it provides to the outside world, you're probably beginning to see why a comprehensive strategy and program for IT accessibility is necessary.

Again, the technical aspects of IT accessibility are relatively well understood. You can draw from a wide body of literature of published technical information to make your organization's IT accessible. A huge and growing body of knowledge—books, training, tools, and experts—is available on how to develop and test for accessibility. However, little information exists about how to establish the governance, business, and organizational structure to facilitate access to IT, whether for the public or another business.

Why is information so lacking in this important and strategic area of IT? After all, the need to make IT accessible started to become a prominent issue around 1998, with the creation of US federal procurement regulations for IT. Ensuring that IT is accessible has been relatively slow for several reasons. Initially, these included the following:

- Lack of awareness or knowledge of IT accessibility
- Lack of awareness of how noncompliance negatively affects a company's performance in the marketplace
- Inconsistent consideration and enforcement in government contracts
- Technical skills and tools that were not readily available

Today, the level of awareness is much higher because of the greater incidence and visibility of lawsuits alleging IT inaccessibility. However, the IT industry is still self-regulating and, with a few exceptions, not doing a very good job of it. Although the industry takes these lawsuits seriously, the impact has not been significant enough to evoke needed changes. Companies pay lip service to IT accessibility by reporting on compliance. Some companies publish Voluntary Product Accessibility Templates, or VPATs, for their products. Unfortunately, most accessibility professionals who use VPAT information to analyze and confirm product accessibility information have found that, except for those filed by a few highly experienced IT companies, many VPATs are inaccurate or simply not credible. Because enforcement is not stringent, many companies do not feel compelled to invest in IT accessibility. Hiring or contracting for technical expertise in accessibility is typically no longer an obstacle; however, the continuous invention of new software technologies creates challenges, for reasons that I will discuss later.

As a manager of design teams developing human-centered hardware and software at IBM for twenty years, I was exposed to IT accessibility fairly early. I first encountered it when I was the manager of one of IBM's elite "Design Centers," a multidisciplinary team of highly creative industrial designers, graphic designers, and human factors engineers. At that time, little existed in the way of industry-wide accessibility regulations or design standards. IBM had its own guidelines for ergonomics, which then included some criteria for people with mobility challenges. For example, the company made sure that system and workstation controls and indicators were visible, readable, and accessible from wheelchair height. At one point, I inherited a software project related to accessibility that never made it to fruition but exposed me to the world of software accessibility. I learned about some of the early work-related standards in accessibility, such as "sticky keys," which allow someone using a mouth stick to perform a task that usually requires simultaneous key presses (ctrl-alt-delete, for example). I also learned that JAWS (job access with speech) was not just a scary movie.

In the late 1990s, I thought it wise to learn about software, so I took a management job in user interface design and development for one of IBM's primary operating system platforms, AIX (IBM's version of UNIX). In addition to creating full-function graphical user interfaces, we had to make them accessible, because IBM's government programs office in Washington, D.C., had already been analyzing the implications and risks of the new federal procurement regulations (Section 508 of the Rehabilitation Act of 1973, as amended in 1998), requiring that all IT purchased by the federal government be accessible. The changes took effect in 2000.

IBM was already a leader in IT accessibility as a developer and producer of IT accessibility products, particularly in the area of assistive technology—products that work in conjunction with IT, enabling people with vision, upper-body mobility, hearing, and even some cognitive disabilities to use software and hardware. Still, the notion of accessibility regulations was daunting, considering the number of products in IBM's portfolio and the significant amount of revenue potentially at risk in the federal sector. To mitigate this risk and ensure continued success in gaining the federal government's business, IBM took on accessibility as a major project.

As I looked for my next management opportunity, I had a conversation about keyboard ergonomics with a former colleague with whom I had worked on several critical customer issues. He had since become an upper-level manager in IBM's Accessibility Center and was looking for someone to run part of his organization. I accepted the position.

My first assignment was to figure out how to integrate accessibility into IBM's development processes, as most of the center's staff came from research areas, with little experience in mainstream development. Initially, they were proceeding in a manner that paralleled the mainstream development process but did not support the tight level of integration needed. Because I had been a software development manager, I knew that making IT accessibility part of the primary product development process was the best way to give accessibility the level of attention it demands. The catch was that integrating IT accessibility into the primary product development process was enormously complex and, therefore, would be difficult to achieve.

I redirected the team and developed a plan, later accepted, for integrating accessibility at key points throughout the complex corporate development process.

In these early stages of ensuring accessibility, IBM focused on the product offerings—the customer side of IT accessibility—and did a good job of providing accessibility services, tools, progress reports, and other materials that would help bring its products into compliance with Section 508 and other standards.

Then, just as product development was moving along relatively well, I started seeing more email correspondence involving other accessibility issues—travel expense reporting tools and personnel directories, for example—in the company's internal IT environment. At that point, internal IT accessibility was not on the radar screen. The focus was the marketplace. It soon became apparent that our employees with disabilities were struggling to perform the simplest IT tasks, ones that other employees took for granted. I determined that the corporate accessibility center needed to address this growing internal problem. I took on this initiative and quickly learned that the internal side of IT accessibility posed even greater challenges and complexities than the product side.

To give you an idea of the enormity of the task, at that point, IBM had thousands of applications running in its environment at any given time throughout the world. Hundreds of new applications were deployed each year, and about the same number were retired. Many were internally developed, whereas others were purchased in their current form or customized to meet IBM requirements. The IT budget was substantial, with tens of thousands of internal application developers around the world. Talk about complexity!

In some places, we were able to use internally the accessibility work already done on the product side, but in other areas, we basically had to start from scratch. All in all, it was quite a ride. Whenever we thought we had a handle on all aspects of IT accessibility on both the customer side and in the internal IT environment, new problems (or opportunities, depending on how you look at it) would arise that required focus and resolution.

It was a continuous learning process for IBM, as well as for me, requiring a great deal of creative problem-solving. Not to say that the job is done: IT accessibility at IBM and many other organizations is still evolving.

After I left IBM and as I was writing this book, I took a job as an accessibility coordinator for a state agency in Texas and then Program Director of Statewide IT Accessibility and had found that some state agencies had already done a sizable amount of work on IT accessibility. As I began to investigate, however, I saw that a lot of elements were still missing. Piecemeal approaches had been taken as agencies gained experience but lacked strategic goals or detailed execution plans for transformation. I began developing these for the sharing them with other agencies as best-practice models for adoption.

1.3 **ABOUT THIS BOOK**

This book draws on the experience I acquired while managing and performing large-scale accessibility transformations for seventeen years in both the private and public sectors and is written in the hope that others may benefit from my experience. The book

- Provides straightforward guidance for those ready to embark on this rewarding journey but have little knowledge of how to approach it
- Fills the large void between the technical and management sides of IT accessibility
- Provides an architecture and framework for the successful integration of accessibility criteria at primary, critical points so that they become woven into the fabric and culture of the organization

Whether your organization is in the public or private sector, local or global, small or large, the concepts, principles, and means of implementation recommended here will apply to you.

To help translate IT accessibility from the abstract to the tangible, I have randomly placed what could be considered "real-world" scenarios throughout the first half of the book. They are designed to bridge the gap between the concepts of IT accessibility and how accessibility issues directly affect people with disabilities and the organization.

These scenarios consider how accessibility issues impact employees in multiple areas of an organization: human resources personnel, product managers, salespeople, legal officers, chief information officers, line managers, top-level executives, procurement experts, and more. Similar scenarios could occur in any organization, public or private, with little or no warning, either because no one was paying attention to IT accessibility or because no one regarded noncompliance as a significant risk to the enterprise.

This second edition is meant to provide updated information on the state of IT accessibility as it has evolved since the original publication, across several pertinent areas. I hope that you find this new information useful.

CHAPTER 1

AN OVERVIEW OF IT ACCESSIBILITY

When I was a young industrial designer in the mid-1980s, I was in Germany on business when I attended a presentation by another industrial designer who was working on a new family of automatic teller machines (ATMs). Like all good industrial designers, he gave a thorough explanation of the rationale and research findings used to develop the final product family and the features and functions of his designs. As he moved through the presentation, I noticed that the height of all the freestanding ATMs was designed to accommodate a standing user but could not accommodate a user in a wheelchair. Afterward I asked him how a person in a wheelchair could use the machine. He politely and seriously responded, "This is not a requirement of the design, because people in wheelchairs are very poor and don't have money; therefore, they don't have need of ATM machines." I was floored. At that time, however, at least in Germany, no policy or law required that such IT equipment be accessible to people with disabilities.

1.1 ACCESSIBILITY ISSUES: A BRIEF HISTORY

Until the mid-1990s or so, the term *accessibility* was strictly associated with the physical world: the ability of people with mobility impairments to gain access to public places. Accessibility was manifested mostly in such architectural features as curb cuts, ramps and safety rails, visual warnings, Braille instructions, and the like. Modifying the existing physical environment was costly, and not many businesses and public agencies were interested in making the modifications needed. The lack of interest probably came down to the same cost-benefit analysis performed by IT-accessibility naysayers: "The number of people who need these physical accommodations doesn't justify the cost." To ensure that people with disabilities were granted equal access to the physical environment, many countries had to enact laws and establish regulations over several decades.

And, until the mid-1990s, only a handful of companies were interested in making IT accessible. Most of this interest lay in producing assistive technologies (AT) for providing access to IT for people with upper-body mobility impairments. However, several smaller companies focused on addressing the needs of users with other physical or sensory challenges, such as visual or auditory impairments. One large corporation, IBM, recognized much earlier the need for providing access to the IT environment and began developing and producing assistive technologies as early as the 1950s and 1960s: Braille typewriters, telephone-teletype (TTY) technologies, text-to-speech products, and more. IBM's efforts, and the efforts of other large IT companies, were not directly related to revenue. Their motivation was rooted in a sense of social responsibility and philanthropy, both of which were already ingrained in IBM corporate culture. This seemed to be true of small AT producers as well, although their compliance was also driven by their personal needs for assistive technologies.

In the late 1990s, however, the motivation for providing IT accessibility changed dramatically, thanks to new legislation: Section 508 of the Rehabilitation Act of 1973, which required accessibility compliance for all IT purchased by US government agencies and the Postal Service. The amendments required that all IT purchased by federal agencies comply with specific accessibility criteria defined in the law.

The amended law made accessibility of information technology a business imperative—at least for those companies that sold IT to federal agencies. Soon after Section 508 took effect, many state and local agencies, as well the governments of other countries, began considering and adopting similar laws and regulations. (See the Reference Information section at the end of the book for a list of countries and agencies that mandate IT accessibility.)

1.1.1 RECENT DEVELOPMENTS

International technical standards began to evolve around the same time that the United States introduced IT accessibility policy and regulations, beginning with the amendments to Section 508. Most notable was the Web Content Accessibility Guidelines, Version 1.0 (WCAG 1.0), which was part of the Web Accessibility Initiative (WAI) begun by the World Wide Web Consortium. This standard defined specific accessibility criteria for making web pages and websites accessible. (The amendments to Section 508 apply to all IT software and hardware, not just the web.) The latest version of this standard at the time of this writing is WCAG 2.3, which replaced the older versions.

Both corporate and government communities have engaged in considerable discussion of international IT standards, such as WCAG 2.0 and higher, and how they should be implemented and enforced. Third-party IT accessibility certification is one method of enforcement that is already in use in Europe thanks to nongovernmental organizations (NGOs) that advocate for people with disabilities. Whether or how such certification programs should be implemented remains controversial.

The amendments to Section 508 took effect almost twenty years ago, but progress toward compliance has been inconsistent and slow. While much progress has been made, there is still a continued exclusion of people with disabilities from IT in the workplace and from the value, enjoyment, and benefits of access to the World Wide Web and other forms or IT.

The US Department of Justice (DOJ) has recognized this problem and is working to remedy it in two ways.

First, on July 26, 2010, the DOJ Civil Rights Division issued an Advanced Notice of Proposed Rulemaking (ANPRM) to the Federal Register that stated:

> The Department of Justice is considering revising the regulations implementing title III of the Americans with Disabilities Act (ADA) in order to establish requirements for making the goods, services, facilities, privileges, accommodations, or advantages offered by public accommodations via the Internet, specifically at sites on the World Wide Web (Web), accessible to individuals with disabilities. The department is also considering revising the ADA's title II regulation to establish requirements for making the services, programs, or activities offered by state and local governments to the public via the Web accessible. The department is issuing this advance notice of proposed rulemaking (ANPRM) in order to solicit public comment on various issues relating to the potential application of such requirements and to obtain background information for the regulatory assessment the department must prepare if it were to adopt requirements that are economically significant according to Executive Order 12866.

There were many public responses to the ANPRM, but not a lot of publicly visible progress regarding publishing a final rule; however, there was activity within the DOJ as they analyzed the potential positive and negative impacts of publishing such a rule. Then, in 2016, the DOJ withdrew the ANPRM and published a Supplemental Advanced Notice of Proposed Rulemaking (SANPRM) referencing Title II (state and local government) entities only and seeking additional, highly detailed information from the public. It is thought that a Title II rule will be published sometime in 2018, but in 2017, the proposed rule was put on the inactive list, so whether a rule will ever see the light of day is anyone's guess. However, the lack of formal regulations by the DOJ does not mean that Title II and Title III entities are not subject to the Americans with Disabilities Act (ADA). It still applies, but there is still no technical standard written into the regulations for entities to comply with, creating some confusion in the US IT world.

On a more positive note, the DOJ has taken the position through various lawsuits in which it has been involved, and in the original 2010 ANPRM, that websites are considered places of public accommodation and therefore subject to Title II and Title III of the ADA. It should be noted that this DOJ position has not always been fully recognized in some courts/states, but it appears that in more recent cases across the country courts have been more often in agreement with this position, resulting in an increasing number of rulings in favor of plaintiffs.

In Europe, the European Parliament and the Council of the European Union issued Directive 2016/2102/EU in late 2016 to make public sector websites and mobile applications more accessible across the European Union. It also uses WCAG 2.0 AA as its technical standard, integrating it into EN 301 549 (accessibility requirements suitable for public procurement of ICT products and services in Europe), further harmonizing around this international standard. Many other countries, states, cities, and regions have adopted or are adopting WCAG 2.0 AA as well, but some are also developing their own accessibility standards, which may not be fully harmonized with WCAG. Although it is good news for people with disabilities that these entities are implementing standards for their accessibility programs, it can create some real challenges for industry when accessibility criteria vary from standards such as WCAG. These variations may or may not have merit, but they create a lot of upheaval as organizations try to develop products and services for international markets.

To ensure consistency of accessibility implementation across the world, committees at the national and international level are working to promote harmonization around key standards for IT accessibility. An example of this is US Section 508, which now references WCAG 2.3AA as its new technical standard.

IT accessibility standards and regulations such as WCAG apply mostly to product or service offerings or web information and commerce—in short, the business-to-business and business-to-consumer areas as well as public/private sector organizations to their employees. (Not complying with these standards carries varying degrees of business risk for an organization.)

Many countries also have enacted antidiscrimination laws and regulations that protect the rights of people with disabilities, ensuring them equality and inclusion in society. The Americans with Disabilities Act, the Accessibility for Ontarians with Disabilities Act in Canada, Disabilities Discrimination Act in the United Kingdom, Law of the People's Republic of China on the Protection of Disabled Persons, and similar measures have been enacted or are pending throughout the world. Most of these include, or are moving to include, language about accessibility of information technology and the associated technical standards.

There is a wealth of information available online that encompasses the specifics of IT accessibility standards, regulations, and other aspects. Gaining a good understanding of them will allow your organization to effectively and legally conduct business in the markets and geographic areas it serves. Interpreting these regulations and their applicability is a job for those versed in disability law and technical standards.

1.2 ACCESSIBILITY AND THE BOTTOM LINE

You may be wondering what all these standards and disability laws have to do with your enterprise's business and internal IT environment. Simply put, these can affect an organization's ability to sell products or provide information or services in markets where IT accessibility regulations and standards are required or highly desirable.

Now that the US DoJ and regulatory bodies in other countries have taken the position that websites are places of accommodations, there has been a dramatic increase in the number of complaints around IT accessibility. These laws are enacted to put people with disabilities on a level playing field with those without disabilities, which is, in fact, enabling the disabled.

Providing IT access to people with disabilities cannot happen without technical enablement. As a result, IT accessibility standards and disability laws are becoming much more intertwined.

As I mentioned earlier, varying degrees of technical challenges are associated with technical enablement for IT accessibility. This can mostly be summed up in what is called the accessibility technology gap. The graph that follows helps articulate the concept and the difficulty of developing solutions to this problem.

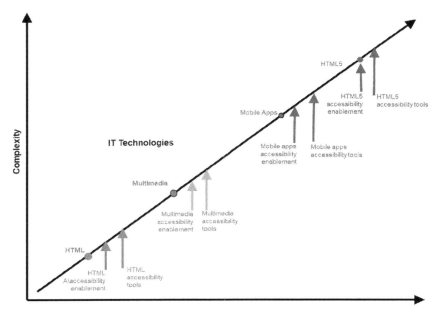

Fig. 1. Graph charting complexity over time

Figure 1 depicts what I consider to be a chronology of web accessibility, the technical challenges faced as the web evolves through innovation:

1. A new technology is invented. Accessibility is not a consideration in the innovation process.
2. The value of the new technology is recognized, and adopters begin to develop it.
3. As adoption increases, so does awareness of the lack of accessibility, which is challenged by regulations or users who require accessibility-enabled interfaces.
4. Developers and the technology creators may take on the task of figuring out how to make the technology accessible.
5. Subject-matter experts train and educate the IT community, but development and testing are all done manually, as tools don't yet exist to facilitate making the technology accessible.
6. If the demand is large enough, development and testing tools are designed to facilitate enablement.
7. By the time the tools are rolled out, the world has begun moving to the next great technology, and the cycle begins again.

As you can see, accessibility enablement of technology has tended to lag behind the adoption of the innovation, creating a persistent gap between the adopting of new technology and the availability of a version that is accessible, or compliant to accessibility technical standards. This is an important consideration when architecting technology platforms and selecting developer/authoring tools to create products and solutions. I will discuss this aspect in more detail in the chapters that follow.

SCENARIO 1: **RECRUITING ONLINE**

Corporation X had just completed the deployment of a large new web application for recruiting new employees and managing job candidates' applications; the program was purchased from Company A, which developed the product. Both Company A's and Corporation X's studies indicated that this system would offer significant advantages over the previous, mostly manual, processes in cost savings, productivity, and candidate quality. Shortly after deployment, Corporation X received an email from Cynthia, a highly talented but frustrated visitor to the new site. Cynthia had tried to search and apply for jobs at Corporation X but couldn't because she is blind and the new website and recruiting tool was not accessible. After several unsuccessful attempts to contact recruiters in Corporation X's human relations department, she sent an email to the main Corporation X address that, after a week or so, finally found its way to the recruiters. Cynthia identified herself as blind and requested help in searching and applying for jobs at Corporation X. However, now that the new online recruiting tool had been fully deployed, Corporation X had already eliminated its manual processes and reassigned the personnel who did this work. A few days after receiving Cynthia's note, a representative of Corporation X contacted Cynthia and told her that someone would get back to her soon to take her application by phone. In the meantime, Cynthia posted her issue on an Internet forum for the blind, frequented by a large international population interested in exchanging information about technical issues, HR policy, and other workplace issues relevant to disabilities.

Also, nearly simultaneously, Kevin, a blind Corporation X employee working in the department responsible for processing candidate information from the new website, determined that he could no longer do his job because the internal side of the application was also not accessible. After reading Cynthia's posting on the Internet forum, Kevin raised this issue as well.

Shortly after Cynthia's posting attracted a few more comments, an attorney from a well-known advocacy group contacted her about her problem. Soon a class-action lawsuit alleging discrimination was filed against Corporation X.

You can probably guess what ensued: multiple lawsuits, finger pointing, unplanned development and deployment activity to provide accessibility, public-relations damage control, executive focus on resolving the problems, and legal costs. Wow. Who knew?

Corporation X was not aware of the accessibility status of the new application when it purchased it, and had never asked, because no one thought about it, including Company A, when it developed the application.

IT ACCESSIBILITY TECHNICAL ENABLEMENT VERSUS BUSINESS TRANSFORMATION

The first order of business in understanding the transformational aspects of IT accessibility is obtaining a clear understanding of the difference between the technical side of accessibility and the business integration side. Although I will touch on aspects of IT accessibility development and testing throughout, I will cover them only within the strategic context of IT accessibility, not at a technical level.

2.1 TECHNICAL ENABLEMENT

The technical enablement of IT accessibility is a critical element of concern, and the technical aspects of making IT accessible or compliant to accessibility technical standards can be challenging.

Whether IT is internally developed by your organization or a third party, there are tools are available to facilitate the development of accessible IT. Therefore, the important question is "Does my development community or third-party supplier use these tools and have the skills to create accessible IT?" This is a legitimate technical question to be asked and answered at the inception of any IT project.

One goal of this book is to help ensure that such questions surface as a matter of process and protocol; they cannot be overlooked.

Issues regarding IT accessibility have been around for a while, but they have only recently surfaced in the mainstream for reasons I will discuss later. A growing number of skilled individuals and a large body of technical knowledge exist on the topic and are available if and when an organization chooses (or is required) to provide IT accessibility or to enable for accessibility.

If your organization is already engaged in enabling technical accessibility at some level, you've already begun what will be a transformational journey. Someone in your organization recognized the importance of IT accessibility to your business or service sectors and has taken appropriate steps to make IT accessibility happen.

If your organization has already developed and shipped accessible IT for the first time, for either a large or small project (such as software or website), either for internal use or as an external product or service, how did it go? Was it smooth sailing, or was it a painful experience?

I would surmise that if you were engaged in the project at a high level (management) and you felt as if accessibility was a slam dunk, your team may have been overly optimistic about it as they reported project status. (After all, a prettier version of reality is usually the way something is painted for higher-level management, right?)

2.2 BUSINESS TRANSFORMATION

As is generally the case, the first attempt at something is usually the hardest, and your organization probably learned a lot about making IT accessible at the technical enablement level: what the job required, points of success, failures to avoid repeating, how schedules or quality were affected, and so on. After this initial experience, the process should be somewhat easier the next time around, shouldn't it? What steps will your organization take to analyze gaps in their processes, and record lessons learned so that the next time around is relatively pain free?

Let's say that next month a team operating in a different location and department of the organization is planning to kick off an important project similar to the one recently made accessible. Resources are invested, and the project is executed "successfully" and according to schedule, with one exception: accessibility was never part of the project.

What went wrong? Here are a few possibilities:

- No one was aware of the requirement for accessibility. The project leader considered it to be optional—a bonus rather than a requirement.
- No one was aware of the previous project or of its having been made accessible. "Sorry, I was just hired and don't know anything about previous projects or accessibility."
- No knowledge or skill transfer took place between the project team that made the first project accessible and the current team. "We disbanded the team after the project was complete."
- Documentation featuring lessons learned from the previous project was not integrated into the organization's development or business processes. "We didn't have time for a post-project 'debriefing.' We were already focused on a new, totally different project!"
- Awareness of the requirement was made too late to be addressed. "The project needed to be accessible? Well, it's too late now—we'll do it next time." No one person is responsible for overseeing accessibility issues. "We thought accessibility was being done by everyone."
- Employees with skills in IT accessibility were reassigned, unavailable, or left the organization. "If it wasn't for that layoff last month …"

- There are no policies or objectives on IT accessibility at an organizational level. "I'm just sticking to the existing development process, and I don't see anything about accessibility."

And the list goes on. Like a traffic cop stopping a speeder, I've heard all the excuses.

The point is this: making one or two IT offerings accessible in a select area of an organization in no way guarantees that IT will henceforth be made accessible consistently and repeatedly throughout the organization. Doing this requires a strategic, holistic approach.

2.3 BECOMING AN IT ACCESSIBLE ORGANIZATION

To mitigate the risk and cost associated with accessibility issues by resolving them consistently and permanently, the organization itself must become attuned to the need for accessibility. This awareness must cross organizational "pillars" and weave itself into the very culture of the organization. An overall policy must be created, along with governance models, organizational structure, means of measuring progress, accountability, process integration or new process development, accommodations methods, training and education at various levels for various audiences, and more.

Such an approach is very different from changing the technology to make IT accessible, although that process is a subset and by-product of organizational enablement. Organizational enablement is synonymous with transforming a business so that it thinks about accessibility at all the appropriate points where IT accessibility may play a role. You may be asking if all this is necessary.

The next several chapters should provide an answer.

SCENARIO 2: **THE WEB CONFERENCE**

Joe is a deaf employee at a medium-size government agency with multiple offices and many telecommuters. Today, the agency director is holding a web conference to present information of great significance to all agency employees. Joe works from home and enters the web conference. He watches the agency director speak but is unable to understand what she is saying because the presentation is not captioned in real time. Joe sends a note to his HR partner informing him of the issue and asks whether a transcript is available; it is not. The HR partner commits to having a transcript made for Joe by an external transcription company, to be available within a week.

In the meantime,, the agency's offices are buzzing about the information given at the conference—but Joe can glean only a bit at a time from conversations with his peers online while he waits for the transcript. Joe is extremely frustrated and disappointed by the apathetic response from HR. He feels disenfranchised and isolated, and he finds the agency's response to this problem unacceptable. He writes a letter to the agency director expressing deep dissatisfaction with the insensitive exclusion of the hearing impaired from the timely delivery of key information.

The agency director sends Joe a personal apology and assures him that this problem will not recur. The director reprimands the organizer of the web conference.

About three months later, the director leaves the agency. The new director brings her own communications staff with her and prepares to deliver an important address to employees—again, as a web conference.

Do I need to tell you what happened? There was no record of the informal interaction between Joe and the former director, and no procedure or process has been put in place to ensure inclusiveness of the hearing impaired. As in scenario 1, a disenfranchised individual, and the potential for a lawsuit is a probable result.

CHAPTER 3

THE CASE FOR ACCESSIBILITY

To fully appreciate the case for IT accessibility, it's useful to take a step back and look at some powerful demographics. According to "The Missing Link: Financing the Industry," a 2007 paper by Barry K. Fingerhut of Synconium Partners,

- Of the world's population, 16 to 18 percent live with some kind of disability, including disabilities related to aging.
- Ten percent of the world's population (more than six hundred million people) lives with life-altering disabilities (vision, hearing, speech, cognition, and mobility).
- Two-thirds of people with disabilities live in developing countries.
- Fifty-four million people in the United States live with disabilities.
- Disability is a key driver of poverty: 70 percent of blind people in the United States are unemployed.
- The US Department of Labor estimates that people with disabilities have an aggregate annual income of nearly $700 billion, including $175 billion in discretionary spending power.

- Between 2011 and 2031, the phenomenon of aging baby boomers will cause the various markets of consumers with disabilities to converge and expand dramatically. Older adults experience greater incidence of disability and "ease of use" issues. According to the US Census Bureau, 14 million older Americans (41.9 percent of the total older adult population) have one or more disabilities. The US Department of Labor reported in 2004 that 36.3 million people (12 percent of the total population) were older than sixty-five. This group is expected to grow to 71.5 million people (20 percent of the total population) by 2030. US adults older than fifty are estimated to have more than $1.7 trillion in discretionary spending power and $17 trillion of net worth.

These demographics have a profound impact on society and information technology, particularly as accessibility policy evolves throughout the world.

Perhaps you are thinking, "Two-thirds of people with disabilities reside in developing countries? I don't sell anything there, so accessibility is not a priority for my organization."

Are you sure? Many developing countries are or are becoming world suppliers of low-cost goods and services. If your organization decides to open a call center in Zimbabwe because it offers the most competitive cost of service on the market, will your company be able to provide the tools and infrastructure necessary to hire and support employees with disabilities there? If not, what will the implications be for your organization? Will you face fines for noncompliance with Zimbabwe's hiring regulations concerning the disabled or for the use of IT that violates that country's accessibility law? Will your company lose its competitive advantage if it chooses not to put the call center there because of these issues?

As you can see, even seemingly irrelevant disability issues can pose major challenges to your organization. The bigger the issue, the higher the cost—financially and socially—to resolve it.

But the case for IT accessibility isn't just about avoiding pitfalls. As IT accessibility matures, the positives will outweigh the negatives. The case for IT can be divided into two main areas of justification: *managing risk* and *creating inclusiveness and business value*.

3.1 **MANAGING RISK**

3.1.1 **IN THE MARKETPLACE**

As I noted earlier, the global IT marketplace has seen a significant increase in the implementation of regulations, standards, and policies concerning accessibility. Quite simply, the less your organization's IT complies with these accessibility regulations, standards, and policies, the greater the risk it assumes in the global IT environment.

Let's say your enterprise has developed a product and is bidding that product for a contract with a federal agency; accessibility compliance is a requirement of the contract. Your offering is not compliant, but the product of competitor for the contract is. Assuming that your product and your competitor's product are relatively equal in price and performance, the contract will likely be awarded to the business that has the compliant (or more compliant) offering. The decision may be based on regulatory enforcement or preference (government agencies may prefer to manage their own internal or external risk).

Let's take that example a step further. Consider a company that plans to make a large bid with many products and services—some are compliant, some aren't—packaged together as a "solution." The primary competitor's solution is either nearly fully compliant or contains key elements that are compliant, such as those pieces that would be used by a large population (a large self-service portal, for example), in contrast to those with a small subset of specialized users (a complex system admin console, for example).

Neither you nor your competitor has a fully compliant solution, but, again, all things being equal, the more accessible solution will win the bid.

These examples are equally applicable to sales between businesses, particularly when customers understand the importance of accessibility and the risk to their business posed by the procurement of non-accessible products or solutions.

Clearly, a lack of attention to accessibility can affect sales and revenue. If an enterprise has non-accessible products, the degree of revenue risk can be predicted based on a good understanding of an organization's customer and regulatory requirements. The projected revenue losses can be used to as rationale that justifies investment decisions around accessibility. What's much more difficult to predict, however, is the collateral damage of knowingly or unknowingly providing non-accessible offerings.

Let's take a look at a high-visibility case of a large retail corporation's website that was inaccessible to a consumer. What follows is an excerpt from the detailed press release previously posted on the website of Disability Rights Advocates):

National Federation of the Blind v. Target

On February 6, 2006, Bruce F. Sexton, Jr., a blind Californian, and the National Federation of the Blind (NFB) filed suit against Target, alleging that its website was not accessible to people with disabilities using screen access technology. (Two other individual plaintiffs, Melissa Williamson and James P. Marks, were later added to the complaint.) Screen access technology (such as JAWS for Windows by Freedom Scientific and WindowEyes by GW Micro) converts documents, web pages, and other text on the computer screen into synthesized speech or Braille, depending on the preference of the user. If Web sites are improperly coded, however, they cannot be read by screen access technology, and blind people cannot access the functionality of the site. The lawsuit alleged that Target had not made the minimum changes necessary to its website to make the site compatible with screen access technology and to allow blind users to access the site to purchase products, redeem gift cards, find Target stores, and perform other functions available to sighted customers. The NFB alleged that this violated the Americans with Disabilities Act, the California Unruh Civil Rights Act, and the California Disabled Persons Act. On October 2, 2007, Judge Marilyn Hall Patel of the Federal District Court for the Northern District of California certified the case as a class action on behalf of two classes of plaintiffs: a nationwide class of "all legally blind individuals in the United States who have attempted to access Target.com and as a result have been denied access to the enjoyment of goods and services offered in Target stores" and a California subclass of "all legally blind individuals in California who have attempted to access Target.com." The agreement that [was] reached [in 2008] by the NFB and Target settles the action as to both of these classes[:]

Terms of the Agreement

- Target has, in consultation with the National Federation of the Blind, determined the steps that need to be taken to make its website accessible to the blind, and incorporated NFB's recommendations into Target's internal guidelines for web accessibility.
- The National Federation of the Blind will monitor Target's progress in making the Target website accessible; provide training to Target employees responsible for its website; and analyze complaints of guests at Target.com regarding the accessibility of the website, and, if necessary, help Target to address those complaints.
- By February 28, 2009, Target.com will be fully accessible—meaning that from that point forward, all information and transactions available to sighted people on Target.com will be fully accessible to blind people with a substantially equivalent ease of use.
- When Target has taken all necessary steps to make its Web site accessible, the National Federation of the Blind will grant Target.com its Nonvisual Access (NVA) Certification, and Target may display the NFB-NVA Web Certification seal on Target.com.
- Target will place $6 million in an interest-bearing account to be paid to members of the California class who submit valid claims. Each claimant will receive $3,500 or an equal pro rata share of this damages fund, depending on the number of claimants and the availability of funds. Individuals may make up to two claims based on separate incidents for a total of $7,000.

- Target will pay $20,000 to a nonprofit corporation set up by Bruce Sexton, the original named plaintiff, for the purpose of establishing the California Center for the Blind, a rehabilitation and training center for blind individuals.
- The National Federation of the Blind is entitled to reasonable attorney's fees and costs, but the exact amount of said fees and costs has not yet been determined.

Domino's Pizza, LLC v. Robles, Guillermo

Another very recent and high visibility case is occurring during the writing of this book: Domino's Pizza, LLC v. Robles, Guillermo case.

It involves a blind individual who sued Domino's because its website was not accessible to the blind. Domino's, rather than just fixing their website(s) argued that the ADA did not apply to websites, for various reasons, and that there were other ways for a blind customer to sufficiently interact with the company to order food.

A lower court for Domino's was appealed to the The Ninth Circuit, which held that Title III of the ADA covers both mobile applications and websites with a connection (nexus) to a physical place of public accommodation.

Domino's then elected to take the case to the US Supreme court; however, the court decided not to hear the case. This was considered a major victory for the disabled community and disability advocates, but the case is not closed. It now goes back to Federal District Court in California for further proceedings. The hope is that the Ninth Circuit decision will be upheld, of course, but stay tuned.

A few other recent examples of interest that led to lawsuits, including some where the Department of Justice intervened on behalf of plantiffs:

- Netflix: lack of closed captioning for streaming video as a violation of the ADA
- Harvard and MIT MOOC: Failing to caption online courses

- Winn Dixie: inaccessible website
- Bag'n Baggage: inaccessible website

As I stated earlier, there has been a significant increase in the number of IT accessibility lawsuits, up 37 percent from 2016 to 2017. This includes what might be considered accessibility trolling law firms that use accessibility scanning tools to determine the accessibility levels of many, random public and private-sector websites, sending demand letters to organizations whose websites had accessibility issues.

3.1.2 **INTERNAL IT**

Now let's turn to an organization's internal environment. Generally speaking, lack of accessibility may not affect revenue directly, but it may hurt the enterprise's public image in ways that can be every bit as detrimental.

Accessibility of internal IT is a workplace issue, with ramifications that typically involve violations of disability law (such as the Americans with Disabilities Act). Therefore, litigation is probably the greatest area of risk for an organization to consider as it seeks to accommodate its employees with disabilities.

As I noted in chapter 1, some internal accessibility issues can be detonators for bombs that have been silently ticking away. The result is likely to be a plethora of legal problems that can also turn into a public relations nightmare and can cost an organization serious money in legal fees, productivity loss, and remedy expenses. It's important to recognize that a single complaint may seem isolated and containable, but communities of individuals with disabilities are close-knit; they share information generously and candidly, particularly within their specific disability group. They provide one another with technical and moral support in real time, and communication does not end at the organization's or the enterprise's firewall. Every time an issue arises and employees with a disability share a problem or frustration with others in their disability group, or with disability advocacy groups, there is potential for disaster. Like this one (from a National Federation for the Blind press release):

National Federation of the Blind Files Suit for Equal Access

Austin, Texas (February 5, 2007): The National Federation of the Blind and three blind Texas employees filed suit today to enforce a provision of Texas law requiring all information technology purchased by the state to be accessible to blind employees. The suit was brought because the blind cannot use software manufactured by Oracle Systems and used by state employees.

The newly acquired software replaced another software package that had, in large part, been accessible to blind users.

Dr. Marc Maurer, President of the National Federation of the Blind, said: "Access to information technology is critical to success on the job for everyone in the twenty-first century, and this is no less true for the blind than it is for the sighted. The National Federation of the Blind is committed to improving access to all information technologies, and we will take all steps necessary to do so, including litigation."

Tommy Craig, President of the National Federation of the Blind of Texas, said: "The state legislature of Texas recognized the need for equal access for the blind by passing a law requiring it, and it is unconscionable that a state agency is violating that law. The National Federation of the Blind of Texas will not rest until all of the employees of the state of Texas have equal access to all the information they need to function effectively."

The suit, which names as defendants the directors of the Health and Human Services Commission and the Texas Workforce Commission (the agencies for which the blind employees work) and the state's acting chief technology officer, arises from the state's continuing renewal of contracts to purchase Oracle's human resources software and other products, despite the fact that the software cannot be used by blind Texas employees. The plaintiffs have asked a Texas court to require the software to be made accessible to the blind and to require that the state discontinue its purchases of inaccessible software.

3.1.3 **HIRING PRACTICES**

I mentioned at the beginning of this chapter that hiring practices regarding people with disabilities pose an area of risk. Many countries have quotas that require companies to hire certain numbers of disabled people, and companies that don't meet the quotas can be fined. Even companies that work diligently at minority hiring find it challenging to identify and recruit candidates with disabilities who have the skill sets the companies need. In many countries with quotas, it's a bit of the chicken-or-egg dilemma: the country's economic conditions, educational infrastructure, and other issues can mean a limited pool of qualified workers with disabilities, making it difficult to meet specified quotas.

Conversely, if your organization has offices in locations with a large pool of skilled workers with disabilities but the organization lacks the tools, IT accessibility infrastructure, knowledge, or desire to hire these workers, fines could be levied as well.

3.2 **CREATING BUSINESS VALUE THROUGH COMPETITIVE ADVANTAGE**

Now that I've covered the risks, let me talk about the positive side: the business advantages your organization will enjoy when it produces and uses accessible IT.

3.2.1 **IN THE MARKETPLACE**

If having inaccessible IT can cost a company money, the reverse is also true: if a company produces accessible offerings, it can expect rewards. The size of these rewards depends on the markets your organization serves today and plans to serve tomorrow.

First, I'll discuss selling to the public sector globally. Here again, regulations, standards, and policies play a large role, so if your organization serves the public-sector marketplace, odds are that accessibility compliance will be crucial to your ability to win business and effectively serve this audience. While full compliance is the best guarantee of winning business when accessibility compliance is a requirement, there can also be situations in which products or services that are more or most compliant (sometimes documented as "compliant with exceptions") can offer a strong competitive edge— that is, if your partial compliance is significantly stronger than that of the other competitors'. I've even observed bid situations in which neither supplier had an accessible product, but the award went to the supplier that did a better job of documenting the accessibility state of its product. (Note: If the purchaser cannot validate the level of accessibility claimed by the seller based on the documentation provided by the bidding organization, the repercussions can be severe.)

In the private sector, accessibility can lead to increased sales or can yield competitive advantage in several ways.

3.2.2 **INCREASED MARKET SHARE**

Recall the statistics that I listed at the beginning of this chapter that detailed global accessibility, various populations with disabilities, and the spending power these groups represent in the United States. These are big numbers, and they don't even include similar populations in the rest of the world. The maturing population represents a particularly strong demographic for revenue opportunity for the following reasons:

- Individuals are choosing to stay in the workforce longer and will need to remain productive while using IT.
- A tech-savvy aging and/or retired population is increasingly dependent on IT for many aspects of life: managing financial and health interests, socializing and sharing personal information with family and friends, obtaining information, and even developing or managing web-based businesses and hobbies.

We're all well aware of the physical effects associated with aging, including deterioration of vision, hearing, and mobility. By making IT accessible and in compliance with regulations, standards, and policies, an organization will also meet the needs of the aging population.

When a product, service, or other offering is designed with features and functions that benefit all users at all levels of physical ability, it can be deemed "universal design." Universal design not only meets accessibility regulations, standards, and policies, but it also represents an edge over other offerings in marketing and sales that is attractive to consumers.

Example: Universal Design and the Fujitsu Raku-Raku Cell Phone

Fujitsu developed the Raku-Raku cell phone for the Japanese market. Universal design was a key driver for its development.

As part of the development process, Fujitsu gathered information from people with disabilities, universal design experts, and others to develop requirements for this product. The resulting product included a rich set of features and functions that benefit all users, including those with age-related and other disabilities. The features developed and integrated during the life span of the Raku-Raku phone included:

- Large screens with the ability to display large letters
- One-touch programmable buttons for making a call simply by pushing the button
- A "text-to-speech" function for mail and websites
- A "speech-to-text" device for composing mail
- An integrated text-to-speech player for books and the like

As a result of its functionality, more than 80 percent of visually impaired people in Japan use the Raku-Raku phone, and more than 15 million Raku-Raku phones were sold between its debut in 1999 and June 2009.

3.2.3 **WEB SEARCH ENGINE OPTIMIZATION (SEO)**

Accessible web content is now considered a valuable tool as an optimizer for search engines. For the most part, search engines are unable to find information when that information is embedded in a web technology or object that has not been coded for accessibility. A good example is a website image, as many images today are still not accessible to individuals with disabilities. A search engine cannot see or understand anything about the image other than that it is an image, so it can't report anything about it to a search user. If the image were accessible, there would be "alternative text" (a caption) created by the author that would describe the image, making it possible for a search engine to pick up on this alternative text and deliver it in the search results for any user. Similar accessibility advantages apply to other web objects, like Flash content, when properly tagged or transcripted.

3.3 **THE INTERNAL ORGANIZATION**

In addition to mitigating risks, thinking about access to information technology holistically provides benefits to the entire organization. The benefits discussed earlier in regard to an aging workforce apply, of course, but when an organization looks at accessibility from a diversity perspective, the benefits go a lot further.

Productivity gains are one example. Think about the entire tenure of a typical employee: recruitment, relocation, performance evaluation, career management, and job changes.

A lack of processes, procedures, tools, and infrastructure to assist in resolving IT accessibility issues for employees with disabilities over the course of their tenure can translate into a substantial amount of additional time and expense from managers, human relations personnel, information technologists, administrators, and others to resolve an issue. Multiply the additional time and expense by the numbers of employees with disabilities within your organization, and you'll begin to see the problem. Each time a situation arises, the manager and others have to figure out yet again how to resolve the problem. The management chain, the HR team, and work tools used will all be completely different, and no one working to resolve the problem will have information about previous similar experiences. A cost-of-business exercise conducted at one of my former workplaces concluded that the development and management of the right processes and tools can translate into tremendous time and cost savings, and improve productivity for employees with disabilities, their supervisors, HR, and everyone else involved in fixing the problem.

Understanding the needs of your employees with disabilities (who, in many cases are more than willing to provide this information) and providing the opportunity for their full inclusion in the workplace not only increases productivity, it improves morale and reduces attrition among employees with disabilities (which is typically higher than for the general population). IT accessibility provides greater opportunities for these employees' personal growth and for them to contribute to the company.

Here's a bit of US data to illustrate these points:

A study conducted by the Job Accommodation Network (JAN), a service of the US Department of Labor's Office of Disability Employment Policy (ODEP), shows that workplace accommodations not only cost an organization little but also positively affect the workplace in many ways.

Employers who made accommodations for employees with disabilities reported multiple benefits as a result. The most frequently mentioned direct benefits were as follows: (1) the accommodation allowed the company to retain a qualified employee, (2) the accommodation increased the worker's productivity, and (3) the accommodation eliminated the costs of training a new employee.

The most widely mentioned indirect benefits employers received were as follows: (1) the accommodation ultimately improved interactions with co-workers, (2) the accommodation increased overall company morale, and (3) the accommodation increased overall company productivity. The following table gives the percentage of employers who reported experiencing direct and indirect benefits as a result of having made an accommodation.

Direct Benefits	Percent
Retained a valued employee	89%
Increased the employee's productivity	71%
Eliminated costs associated with training a new employee	60%
Increased the employee's attendance	52%
Increased diversity of the company	43%
Saved workers' compensation or other insurance costs	39%
Hired a qualified person with a disability	14%
Promoted an employee	11%

Indirect Benefits	Percent
Improved interactions with co-workers	68%
Increased overall company morale	62%
Increased overall company productivity	59%
Improved interactions with customers	47%
Increased workplace safety	44%
Increased overall company attendance	38%
Increased profitability	32%
Increased customer base	18%

Source: Job Accommodation Network, Office of Disability Employment Policy, US Department of Labor, "Workplace Accommodations: Low Cost, High Impact," Fact Sheet Series, September 1, 2010, Job Accommodation Network, Morgantown, West Virginia, 4.

Indirect benefits also emerge. For example, once an organization has begun to incorporate accessibility in everything it does, it can begin to make its plans public. Such initiatives have high public relations value.

The accessibility initiative is a powerful way for an enterprise to demonstrate its commitment to social responsibility and good corporate citizenship by being inclusive. This will produce a positive public perception of the organization and consequently of the brand.

These first chapters have provided the rationale for adopting an accessibility program within your organization.

3.4 LAST BUT NOT LEAST: ACCESSIBILITY IS A CIVIL RIGHT

While the above-mentioned business incentives are helpful, it is crucial to keep in mind that in the United States and many other countries, IT accessibility is considered a civil right. In the US, the Department of Justice has taken the position that websites are places of public accommodation, therefore are required to be accessible to everyone—including people with disabilities.

This position was stated by the DOJ during the Netflix case:

"The Department is currently developing regulations specifically addressing the accessibility of goods and services offered via the web by entities covered by the ADA. *The fact that the regulatory process is not yet complete in no way indicates that web services are not already covered by title III.*"

Do you think there was a business case that supported this statement? If there was, it would have certainly been externalized by now, right?

For comparison, let's look at accessibility regulations for the built environment (choose a state, province, country, etc.). Were there business cases that justified the cost of fitting new and existing buildings for accessibility? While there were probably numerous impact assessments done, I'm not aware of any use of business cases, *because business case justification is not relevant when dealing with civil-rights issues.*

If you follow this rationale and set a precedent for the accessibility of the built environment, one can see that business case justification may not be the best argument for providing access to ICT. What's different about giving people physical access to a building or a restroom as opposed to all of the services, goods, and information offered on public websites? Civil rights–wise I would argue … nothing.

Before accessibility regulations for the built environment were enacted, entities rarely would have decided to expend financial resources of their own volition for accessibility, because physical accessibility was an expense that they would have rather not incurred and didn't see the need (business case) to incur it. Therefore, if left up to the entities themselves to "do the right thing," very little would have been done, leaving those with disabilities literally out in the cold. To solve this problem, regulations were enacted. While enforcement was and can still be challenging as new situations arise, the initiative has been very successful given the scale of the built environment. In the US, for example, you will rarely encounter a commercial building code that doesn't require full compliance with accessibility laws. Also, oversight and enforcement are fairly strict.

Now, let's turn to the ICT environment. What motivation, other than "doing the right thing," do organizations have for investing (yes, it does require investment) in ICT accessibility? Let's be frank. When comparing the ratio of the number of organizations that develop, sell, or use ICT worldwide to the demonstrated business case and ROI examples for increased revenue and profitability from implementing ICT accessibility over the past ten years, the ratio is pretty darn low.

The same holds true on the cost of litigation when it occurs. Sure, there have been some high visibility cases (mostly settled and not ruled on by judge or jury), but again, in relation to the number of websites organizations in the global ICT environment, there have not been that many; however; there has been a significant surge in such lawsuits recently, creating around 37 percent from 2016 to 2017.

It is becoming increasingly clear that equal access to goods and services, be it physical or electronic, is not a business option; it's a civil right and needs to be addressed to mitigate risk to organizations. The remaining chapters will take you through the establishment of a successful, comprehensive accessibility program.

SCENARIO 3: **USE OF VIRTUAL WORLDS IN BUSINESS**

Judy is a blind employee at a high-tech company. One of the company's key goals is positioning itself as a highly progressive IT company. Therefore, it needs to lead the industry in using cutting-edge technology whenever possible. To advance this message and cultural philosophy, a company executive decides to hold a meeting in a publicly available virtual-world environment to demonstrate how the area he manages is embracing this progressive culture. He invites not only his employees but also several large customers with hundreds of their own employees. However, the virtual world to be used is not IT accessible, so Judy will be unable to attend.

Employees of the invited client companies who have visual or hearing impairments are indignant at being excluded from the event. The executives of the guest companies get an earful, and the commotion quickly reaches the chief executive officer of the host company, who is already experiencing the wrath of his own employees with impairments, including Judy's.

The whole event becomes a huge fiasco. All companies and their managers make profuse apologies. The CEO of the host company, who had developed an investment strategy to transfer more of his organization's services to a virtual environment, has to scrap his plans. He suffers great embarrassment, nearly loses his job, and barely escapes the consequences described in scenario 1, "A Class-Action Lawsuit Alleging Discrimination."

GETTING STARTED

Whether your enterprise has already experienced problems resulting from an IT accessibility–related issue or not, the groundwork for establishing the IT accessibility process is essentially the same. An enterprise affected by an accessibility issue will probably be much more receptive to formally launching an initiative and, depending on the situation, want to move quickly to achieve accessibility.

An enterprise that has not had this experience may proceed more slowly or may even question the need to take on accessibility to any meaningful degree.

Either way, the process of gaining acceptance for an accessibility program within your organization is fundamentally the same. It should include the reasons, methods, and projected costs associated with such an initiative, communicated in a style appropriate for the enterprise. Also, the proposal should be delivered at the highest level of the organization possible, where vision, broad thinking, and business savvy are greatest. Aim too low in the food chain, and mid-level managers will tend to get mired in parochialism and low-level details. There will be plenty of time for all that once things get going.

A highly effective approach is to commission a deliverable—such as a presentation or a document—from subject-matter experts outside and inside the enterprise (if they exist). The deliverable should include information in the following areas:

- A global perspective on current and pending accessibility regulations, standards, and policies in information technology
- Concrete examples of organizations in the public and private sectors that have suffered adverse impacts from IT accessibility issues
- Examples of adverse impacts that have occurred or are occurring within the organization or enterprise
- Concrete examples of where investment in IT accessibility yielded positive financial results or other benefits for the enterprise
- The state of IT accessibility, if known (if not known, that can be a risk in itself), within your organization's specific area of expertise
- Why accessibility is important to your enterprise
- A clearly defined set of accessibility objectives, framework, and high-level execution plan
- Short-term and forward-looking estimates of costs associated with the program
- Recommended next steps

The primary objectives of delivering this presentation to the highest levels of management possible are to

1. Get top executives to understand the need for an accessibility program

2. Gain the commitment of top executives in the form of resources (human and financial)
3. Request or nominate sponsors, or "champions," for the program to help get it rolling

Assuming that the presentation sells top executives on the need for an accessibility program, you will be ready to begin weaving accessibility into the fabric of your organization's systems, processes, and culture.

4.1 IT ACCESSIBILITY POLICY

Developing an accessibility policy is the cornerstone of any organization-wide IT accessibility program. It gives the entire organization a clear, consistent understanding of IT accessibility and how it fits into the organization. The IT accessibility policy provides overarching governance and is the foundation upon which nearly every other aspect of accessibility is based. All subsequent accessibility-related operations will point to or reference this policy in one way or another. It will represent the "big stick" needed to motivate and get things done.

4.1.1 DEVELOPING THE ACCESSIBILITY POLICY

Accessibility policies are as diverse as the organizations and enterprises governed by them. Rather than providing actual examples of policies, I will focus on the key elements of a company's accessibility policy.

A useful and productive way to start is with a review of various published policies from a cross-section of public- and private-sector organizations you feel are relevant to yours. A brief web search of "accessibility policy" will provide many examples of policies, and this research can be an excellent source from which to draw in crafting your policy. Keep in mind, however, that many private-sector enterprises may choose not to publicly disclose their complete policies. They may paraphrase, publish only excerpts, or use completely different language from that which appears in their internal policy documents. Some industries consider accessibility policy to be intellectual property that provides them with a competitive advantage and therefore is not made available to the public.

For example, IBM, considered a leader in IT accessibility, references its accessibility policy at times, known as Corporate Instruction 162 (CI-162 for short), but has never published the policy language publicly in its entirety.

In the public sector, published policies are much more prevalent and rarely withheld from the public.

So, while you may come across publicly available policy language, the phrasing that actually drives and governs accessibility activities within an enterprise may be more detailed and specific. Care must be taken in simply lifting published accessibility policy language—particularly that of private-sector enterprises—as it may not be complete, and the lifting may constitute plagiarism or copyright infringement.

A word about including technical criteria or specific standards in your accessibility policy. These do not need to be part of an overarching policy meant to provide general guidance for operating the organization.

4.1.2 THE POLICY DEVELOPMENT TEAM AND PROCESS

To develop a lasting, meaningful, and appropriate accessibility policy for your organization, a small core team should be organized that combines

- Deep knowledge of accessibility at the IT industry level (probably a consultant)
- Understanding of technical compliance based on current and emerging standards and regulations

- Expertise in policy and governance within the context of the organization's business processes and controls

Members of the core team should have the knowledge and experience to develop a high-level policy document that

- Contains definitions of key words and concepts in the policy
- Is broad in scope and includes all relevant areas of IT
- Provides unambiguous direction and operational guidance
- Includes directives to measure and report results
- Defines responsibilities and accountability
- Includes a procedure for policy exceptions
- References the specific laws, standards, or regulations that the organization may be bound to comply with (optional)
- References supplementary implementation information, such as checklists and development guides for internal and external IT

In addition to establishing this core team, the organization must develop a process for key stakeholders—representatives of areas likely to be affected by the policy—to review and eventually approve drafts of the policy. Of course, if a policy development or review process already exists in your organization, use that. Be sure that all key stakeholders are included, and err on the side of caution: include more rather than fewer. If a stakeholder area is somehow left out of the initial review and approval process, winning acceptance of the policy and the need for IT accessibility from that stakeholder could get sticky, putting the overall program at risk.

The diagram that follows is an example of an accessibility policy development/stakeholder process structure:

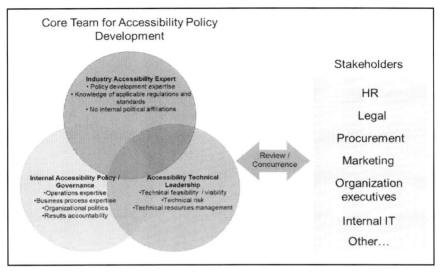

Fig. 2. Accessibility policy formulation diagram

Here are the three main components that make up the core policy development team, including the skills and knowledge needed in each area to ensure that an effective, "balanced" policy is the end result. At various points (at least once) in the policy development process, input and feedback should be obtained from all of the stakeholder areas within the organization. Input should then be factored into the policy formulation. Once completed, all of the stakeholders should formally sign off on the final policy document.

Once the policy has been completed and vetted and has received the appropriate approvals, it can be put to work immediately to help guide the organization as it integrates IT accessibility into everything it does.

4.2 POLICY-DRIVEN ADOPTION FOR ACCESSIBILITY(PDAA): AN ACCESSIBILITY GOVERNANCE MODEL

An organization-wide accessibility policy is, by definition, written at a very high level to provide both broad latitude in its scope as well as some fundamental guidance for the organization, but trying to use it alone without a governance system to set the stage for implementation will be a frustrating ordeal. The development and introduction of a governance system, or model, provides the next level of detail and contains concrete criteria from which to achieve the organization's policy objectives. Governance criteria not only provides this next level of organizational guidance, *but its criteria can be measured.*

Once such governance model that is gaining traction in both industry and governance is policy-driven adoption for accessibility, or PDAA.

PDAA was developed in 2013 though a work initiative by the National Association of State CIOs (NASCIO). It was a collaborative effort with representation from members form ten state and one federal agency. The primary authors of PDAA were myself and my counterparts Jay Wyant, chief accessibility officer for the state of Minnesota, and Sarah Bourne, director of IT accessibility, commonwealth of Massachusetts.

The workgroup objectives were to develop an IT accessibility governance system that could be used consistently from state to state/vendor to vendor.

The idea behind PDAA or any policy-driven governance model is to integrate IT accessibility into the organization's policies in a way that enables them to drive themselves to improve accessibility adoption. Such an approach

- Makes IT accessibility difficult to ignore
- Is not overly prescriptive (tells what, not how)
- Can be governed through non-technical methods
- Can accelerate marketplace innovations in IT accessibility

4.2.1 **PDAA CORE CRITERIA**

Six elements comprise the core criteria for PDAA. Each one is tied to a specific area of organizational operations.

Key areas	Core criteria
Policy creation	1. **Develop, implement, and maintain an IT accessibility policy.** The IT accessibility policy is the foundation on which accessibility programs and initiatives can be built. Without it, accessibility work is tactical and not part of a holistic organization-wide strategy.
Organization	2. **Establish and maintain an organizational structure that enables and facilitates progress in ICT accessibility.** Ensures that ICT accessibility is positioned appropriately within the organization, and accessibility-related position roles and responsibilities are defined across the organization, including the designation of an executive sponsor.
Business process	3. **Integrate ICT accessibility criteria into key phases of development, procurement, acquisitions, and other relevant business processes.** Ensures that ICT accessibility happens in a consistent, repeatable fashion and is not dependent on a specific individual(s) who "carries the torch" for any specific event or project where ICT accessibility is required.
Compliance planning	4. **Provide processes for addressing inaccessible IT.** Ensures that plans are developed to address IT accessibility issues once identified. Examples include corrective actions in project plans, procurement of more accessible IT, and providing alternate means of access to the IT product or service.
Training	5. **Ensure the availability of relevant IT accessibility skills within (or to) the organization.** Ensures that the organization has the skills, tools, or external resources needed to create and maintain accessible IT.
Communication	6. **Make information regarding IT accessibility policy, plans, and progress available to customers.** Providing information about how core criteria numbers 1 through 5 are met gives procurement organizations additional data points on vendors' ability and commitment to IT accessibility beyond just VPAT™ or other technical documentation.

4.2.2 **THE PDAA MATURITY MATRIX**

PDAA Core Criteria can be seen as a valuable set of objectives from which an organization can build an IT accessibility program, but without a way to gauge progress toward achieving those objectives, how does the organization know they have been achieved? To ensure this, a qualitative metric set was also developed to assess maturity and progress of an organization towards meeting the PDAA Core Criteria.

In the PDAA model, maturity is measured along a sliding scale approximated using three phases of maturity:

1. Launch phase
2. Integrate phase
3. Optimize phase

These meaning of these phases is qualified below in the PDAA
Maturity Matrix:

Core criteria	Launch	Integrate	Optimize
1. Develop, implement, and maintain an ICT accessibility policy.	Have an ICT accessibility policy.	Have appropriate plans in place to implement and maintain the policy.	Establish metrics and track progress toward achieving compliance with the policy.
2. Establish and maintain an organizational structure that enables and facilitates progress in ICT accessibility.	Develop an organization-wide governance system.	Designate one or more individuals to be responsible for implementation.	Implement a reporting/decision mechanism and maintain records.
3. Integrate ICT accessibility criteria into key phases of development, procurement, acquisitions, and other relevant business processes.	Identify candidate processes for criteria integration.	Implement process changes.	Integrate fully into all key processes.
4. Provide processes for addressing inaccessible ICT.	Create plans that include dates for compliance of inaccessible ICT.	Provide alternate means of access until the ICT is accessible; implement corrective actions process for handling accessibility technical issues and defects.	Maintain records of identified inaccessible ICT, corrective action, and tracking.
5. Ensure the availability of relevant ICT accessibility skills within (or to) the organization.	Define skills/job descriptions.	Identify existing resources that match up and address gaps.	Manage progress in acquiring skills and allocating qualified resources.
6. Make information regarding ICT accessibility policy, plans, and progress available to customers.	Make launch-level information available.	Make integrate-level information available.	Make optimize-level information available.

4.2.3 **THE PDAA SELF-ASSESSMENT TOOL**

For organizations to understand where they sit within the PDAA Maturity Matrix, a questionnaire was developed. As responses are entered into the questionnaire, the results are tabulated and rendered on a bar graph that illustrates where an organization sits on the phased PDAA Maturity Model continuum, as illustrated below:

Fig. 2a. PDAA assessment results bar

This overall result, as well as the results of the individual responses on the questionnaire, can be used to help understand where progress is being made (or not) so that plans can be formulated and implanted to get the organization to the "optimize" phase.

Note that the PDAA governance model is intentionally written to be very broad, leaving it up to the organization to utilize it as best fits an organization and its culture. There are other IT accessibility maturity/ maturity models from various public- or private-sector entities, some of which are much more detailed and therefore perhaps not as flexible, but whether an organization uses PDAA or another model, using α model is the important point.

The PDAA model also has applicability in organization procurement processes, and this will be covered in a later chapter of the book.

SCENARIO 4: **NEWLY DISABLED EMPLOYEE**

Keith is a highly valued, model employee in the large call center of a major insurance company. Keith is efficient and able to complete his calls within a minimal amount of time. He has one of the highest overall customer-satisfaction ratings in the center. About six months ago, Keith was in a serious accident that resulted in a permanent and complete loss of vision. His managers and coworkers were distraught over Keith's condition, both on a personal level and because his absence affected productivity and satisfaction numbers.

Being the positive and strong individual he is, Keith rapidly took on the task of learning to use a screen reader during his recovery and rehabilitation. (A screen reader is an assistive technology for the blind and visually impaired that reads aloud information on the screen.) Keith was highly confident that he would be able to get back to work, using the screen reader to do his job effectively and efficiently and maintain the same high quality and productivity as before the accident.

Upon returning to work, Keith quickly learned that the nearly all the software that he used as a call-center rep—the scripts, call-logging tools, and other resources—were not accessible, rendering his screen reader, and consequently his ability to do his job, useless. While the company tried to find ways to accommodate Keith so that he could somehow continue in his position, everyone soon realized that it was a futile effort without accessibility built into the call center's expensive tools. Keith, the managers, and human-relations professionals worked to find Keith a job outside the call center where IT accessibility would not be an issue, but it soon became apparent that accessibility had not been a consideration or a recognized requirement when the company upgraded its IT in the past several years. After several attempts at other jobs, Keith was laid off in one of the company's downsizing actions because of his low productivity in the inaccessible IT environment.

Keith contacted a civil rights attorney and filed a discrimination complaint against the company and its managers that eventually became a class-action suit. The suit cost the company financially, its public image suffered, and it lost an employee who had tremendous potential for future leadership in the company.

CHAPTER 5

ORGANIZING IT ACCESSIBILITY

After the organization-wide IT accessibility policy is written, one of the first steps in integrating accessibility into an organization is determining the best area within the organization to effectively manage accessibility. This decision is a strategic one, and by its very nature, it communicates a great deal about the importance of the initiative and its ability to drive the change needed to achieve an accessible enterprise.

5.1 SENIOR MANAGER AS EXECUTIVE SPONSOR

As with any high-level organizational decision, opinions will vary as to where the accessibility project belongs. Arguments for and against the various proposals will range from the pragmatic to the political. An important step is determining which senior manager or managers believe strongly in this initiative, understand that the transition will not be easy, and are willing to champion accessibility for the organization by supporting those responsible for implementation.

Sponsoring and championing this initiative will involve

- Developing and promoting the organization's accessibility policy and governance
- Providing, obtaining, or facilitating funding to get the program going and enable its maintenance and growth over time
- Representing accessibility in mediation or when major accessibility issues become contentious (such issues are inevitable)
- Evangelizing accessibility, both within the organization as well as through external communications channels
- Assisting in the development of mid- and low-level accessibility organizational management structures responsible for implementing, maintaining, and upgrading accessibility

Another important consideration of the executive sponsor role is the level of stability where the executive team and mission reside. Given the dynamics in modern organizations, this stability will go a long way toward allaying doubts within the organization as to the credibility/longevity of the program and illustrate that accessibility is not just another flash in the pan initiative. (Perhaps you were involved in the ISO 9000 quality-certification process for corporations back in the late 1990s. It's a good example of a flash-in-the-pan initiative.)

In December of 2013, Gartner published a press release titled "Gartner Says Companies Should Deploy Technologies to Address IT Accessibility." Within that paper was a recommendation that "suppliers should designate a leadership position, such as a chief accessibility officer, to take the lead in educating the organization and customers on assistive technology," and I have recently seen organizations create this chief accessibility officer (CAO) position.

Depending on the "culture" of an organization, the CAO role may house many of the duties defined in the senior manager/executive sponsor role, or it could even eliminate the need for this role.

From an organizational perspective, it makes sense that the executive sponsor be part of senior management in the selected area where the organization's accessibility project team (and CAO) resides. Having both in the same reporting chain will

1. Greatly assist in resolving issues around initialization of the program
2. Provide continuity of the program over time
3. Provide high-level support when disagreements escalate (which they will)
4. Provide support for appropriate levels of funding and growth as the mission matures

If an organization's management structure is highly matrixed, it may still be preferable to have both the executive sponsor and the organization's accessibility project team in the same area, but it may not be crucial. However, if the organization has a more traditional management structure, choosing the executive sponsor and the team's location within the organization should be a package deal. The key to success, as I discussed earlier, is that high-level executives understand and embrace the importance of accessibility and are willing to champion it. If this doesn't happen, the effectiveness and success of the initiative could be compromised.

5.2 NEUTRAL PLACEMENT OF THE IT ACCESSIBILITY FUNCTION

As discussed in chapter 3, accessibility has the potential to affect many areas of an organization, so when selecting the optimal home for this new broad initiative, you need to consider several key factors:

1. Will it get the care and attention needed over time?

2. Is it positioned to reach across the enterprise?
3. Can it maintain its ability to perform without being subjected to the parochial interests of the organization in which it resides?
4. Will it have the clout to be effective in driving transformation and policy?

That is ... does it have neutral placement?

Selecting the right area requires some critical thinking to get this right.

The table that follows offers a few thoughts on the pros and cons of potential locations for the accessibility team. Because every organization or enterprise and its culture is unique, consider this table a model that you can and should modify according to the specific structure of your business. Such an exercise can be a useful tool in determining the best home for accessibility. This model involves a corporate environment with both product development and internal IT, but it can be adapted to fit any organizational structure.

Location	Pros	Cons
Human resources	Good for driving internal IT, HR policy components, and enforcement; is familiar with the entire enterprise or organization.	Difficult for driving compliance for external products and services.
Compliance	Consistency with other compliance programs; associated and strong ability to govern by means of business controls and audits.	Far removed from technical work and its management; no ownership of or accountability to the product areas affected. Locating accessibility here means locating technical skills in a nontechnical area.

Location	Pros	Cons
Product development	Close integration with development community; strong ability to supply staff with technical skills.	Competing business requirements will make accessibility the victim of trade-offs and marginalization; not likely to focus on internal IT and other affected areas of the organization.
Internal IT	Effective for driving internal IT compliance; potential for strong linkage with HR and other areas of the enterprise.	Considered "infrastructure" and more susceptible to budget and funding fluctuations; will find it difficult to drive accessibility to profit-and-loss areas of the organization.
Corporate or organization-wide operations	Provide ability to reach across the organization and require a level of accountability; the authority of a top-level function of the organization won't be questioned.	Could be viewed as a support function that can be easily dismissed or treated as lower priority by other stakeholder areas; limited accountability for results.

Table 5.1

Once a home has been established, the executive sponsor and key staff can begin to flesh out the accessibility organization and management system for the organization. The organizational structure for instituting and maintaining accessibility will depend on the specific characteristics of the organization, such as

- Size
- Existing organizational structure
- Whether it is public or private
- The nature of its IT (development and sales of products and services versus public services, for example)
- Other factors

5.2.1 **THE CORE: A. CENTRALIZED ACCESSIBILITY FUNCTION**

Once the enterprise has selected an organizational home, the focus can move to which centralized capabilities should be contained within it. Again, the characteristics of the organization will determine what functional departments and disciplines should be included. Depending on the size and nature of the organization and the level of available investment, centralized accessibility can be structured as follows:

1. Separate departments within the centralized accessibility area
2. Integrated as a single multidisciplinary department
3. A combination of separate and integrated, tailored to the specific organization

Important areas that are universally relevant for a centralized accessibility organization include

Policy and Governance

- Develops, maintains, and communicates an organization's accessibility policy
- Tracks external media information on newly identified or pending changes in laws or regulations that will affect accessibility
- Performs periodic policy reviews and develops revision proposals based on changing marketplace and regulatory requirements
- Works with other areas of the centralized accessibility team to analyze changing marketplace and regulatory requirements to understand and address the technical implications

Technical Consulting and Support

- Maintains a critical mass of subject matter experts in accessibility development and testing to provide deep technical consulting services to the organization
- Develops and maintains technical and reference information for use across the organization in implementing accessibility policy
- Develops and provides accessibility technical training for developers, testers, etc.

Accessibility Project Office

- Works with centralized and subunit teams to develop processes and plans to integrate accessibility transformation work throughout the organization
- Develops and uses reporting tools for tracking accessibility compliance progress
- Communicates status of implementation and initiatives to executives and other organization management
- Serves as a focal point for general incoming questions (both external and internal) related to accessibility
- Maintains a database of the organization's accessibility documents, including Voluntary Product Accessibility Templates (VPATs), exceptions, etc.

Business Support

- Marketing communications (public relations, lead generation, and thought leadership)
- Sales support when accessibility is a requirement in bids
- Business development for accessibility portfolio (if it exists or is planned)

5.2.2 **OPERATIONAL FOCAL POINTS**

While having a centralized organization for implementing accessibility is vital to bringing about accessibility transformation, but the size and nature of the organization may be such that centralized accessibility alone may be insufficient to support the sublevels (divisions, functional areas, departments).

Organizations are not static but evolve over time: changes occur in strategic direction, new businesses or business units or agencies are introduced, acquisitions are incorporated, or other changes in the organizational structure occur, some of which may even change aspects of the corporate culture. Such organizational dynamics make relying wholly on a centralized accessibility area less than ideal, as a centralized unit may not be familiar with or have any direct stake in new or peripheral semiautonomous subunits.

Therefore these subunits need to have a degree of autonomy to deal with accessibility within the context of that subunit's mission and act as a liaison to the centralized accessibility program.

Depending on the size and nature of the subunit, "focal points" or "coordinators" should be appointed in a full- or part-time capacity to be responsible for and dedicated to accessibility-related work within these subunits. The focal points or coordinators should report directly within these subunits (preferably at a fairly high level) while maintaining a semiformal or "dotted-line" organizational relationship to the centralized accessibility organization. This should help ensure that the goals and needs of the subunit are aligned and balanced with the overall objectives of the organization.

In very large subunits (with diverse IT areas, for example), there may also need to be additional or second-level subunit focal points that liaison with the subunit focal points or coordinators to ensure that there is adequate balance and focus where needed.

An example of such an organizational model appears below.

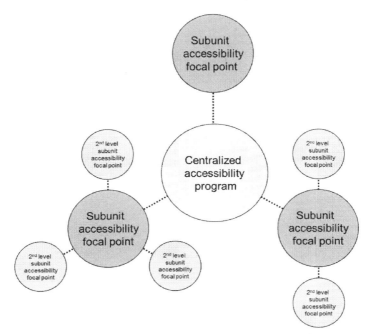

Fig. 3. Diagram of an accessibility organizational structure

5.3 IT ACCESSIBILITY FOCAL POINT OR COORDINATOR: ROLES AND RESPONSIBILITIES

Roles and responsibilities for subunit accessibility coordinators/ focal points will vary from organization to organization, depending on the mission/business of each organization, but there are some roles and responsibilities of these key individuals that should be common. These could include, but not limited to, the following:

Leadership, Guidance, and Consulting

- Acts as the primary contact for/to the organization-level accessibility team
- Provides accessibility leadership and consulting to the subunit and second-level subunits

- Leads the development of subunit and second-level subunit accessibility plans
- Researches and recommends IT accessibility best practices
- Recommends and advises on the integration of IT accessibility criteria for development and testing processes, procedures, resource requirements, and schedules
- Identifies and recommends tools for developing and testing IT accessibility
- Facilitates the IT accessibility exceptions processes when full accessibility cannot be achieved

Ensuring Compliance

- Develops and maintains subunit policies, procedures, guidelines, and tools that support IT accessibility
- Consults with operations and IT procurement staff members to ensure that accessibility requirements are incorporated into subunit IT procurement processes
- Works with staff to develop compliance plans
- Provides guidance on remediation/corrective action plans for inaccessible IT
- Drives resolution of accessibility issues
- Review accuracy and completeness of completed accessibility checklists, VPATs, etc.
- Develops, implements, and maintains a process for the public and staff members to report accessibility issues to the organization

Planning

- Plans, monitors, and coordinates subunit IT accessibility activities
- Develops subunit IT accessibility strategies and implementation plans

Reporting

- Regularly reports IT accessibility status, progress, and other relevant information to management
- Develops administrative reports, studies, research projects, etc., as needed

Training and Promoting

- Builds support for IT accessibility among subunit members and stakeholders through presentations, training facilitation, and consultation on accessibility-related topics
- Identifying subunit and second-level subunit skill gaps and training requirements

5.3.1 ACCESSIBILITY FOCAL POINT OR COORDINATOR: SKILLS REQUIREMENTS

The subunit focal points or coordinators should have a mix of the skills represented here. Keep in mind that the required level of sophistication for each of these skills depends on the nature of the product or services the organization provides.

Skills include the following:

- Understanding of organization IT development processes
- Project management
- IT accessibility technical skills (programming, etc.)
- Negotiation skills
- Familiarity with IT accessibility standards, regulations, and policies
- Strong knowledge of subunit products, services, or processes
- Communications and presentation abilities
- Creative problem-solving

5.3.2 SECOND-LEVEL ACCESSIBILITY FOCAL POINT OR COORDINATOR: ROLES AND RESPONSIBILITIES

Focal points and coordinators for second-level subunit accessibility are very similar to the subunit focal points/coordinators. These individuals should:

- Serve as the primary contact to/for the subunit accessibility focal point or coordinator
- Provide leadership and consulting to the second-level subunit on all aspects of IT accessibility
- Coordinate activities and drive resolution of accessibility issues within the second-level subunit and the subunit
- Lead the development of second-level subunit accessibility and compliance plans
- Provide feedback on progress, issues, and the like to the subunit focal point or coordinator and management
- Identify second-level subunit skill gaps and training requirements
- Participate in subunit and organization-level accessibility activities as identified
- Manage the accessibility exceptions process for the second-level subunit
- Work with second-level subunit teams to develop remediation plans
- Review accuracy and completeness of completed accessibility checklists, VPATs, etc.

5.3.3 SECOND-LEVEL ACCESSIBILITY FOCAL POINT OR COORDINATOR: SKILLS REQUIREMENTS

While this role is also very similar to that of the subunit focal point or coordinator, it has a slightly different mix of skills. Again, the required level of sophistication for each skill depends somewhat on the nature of the product or services the organization provides. This individual needs the following skills:

- An understanding of second-level subunit development and IT management processes
- IT accessibility programming skills (programming, etc.)
- Negotiating skills
- In-depth knowledge of subunit products, services, and processes
- Good knowledge of accessibility standards, regulations, and policies
- Communication and presentation skills

Depending on the organization's size and the nature of its work, the subunit and second-level subunit focal point or coordinator positions could be merged into a single position, in which case, the skills I have defined and the responsibilities would need to be thoughtfully merged as well.

5.3.4 THE ORGANIZATIONAL CROSS-FUNCTIONAL WORKGROUP

While having focal points assigned within each of the units is very important, what formal channels do they have to share valuable information/discuss issues with each other? This is where the concept of an organizational cross-functional workgroup comes in. The primary goal of this workgroup is to facilitate progress in IT accessibility across the organization.

Rather than a workgroup that consists only of IT accessibility professions such as focal points or individuals from the centralized IT accessibility area, this group is an interdepartmental, multidisciplinary team representing stakeholder areas of the organization that require or may be affected by ICT accessibility. Such a workgroup can be extremely valuable, for dealing with accessibility problems that cut across an entire organization and outside the scope/responsibility of any single unit or subunit.

Some examples of this work group's primary mission (or charter, perhaps to be sure it is formalized?) include the following:

- It is a "cross-pollination" vehicle to learn about and share best practices from each other to minimize duplicity of efforts within the organization.
- It identifies organization-wide accessibility roadblocks and issues.
  - o Proposes plans and develops solutions/plans to resolve them
- It documents/reports progress and issues to senior leadership soliciting their assistance when needed.
- It communicates work initiatives and accomplishments throughout the organization (as appropriate).
- It communicates through the chain of command when needed.

Below are some examples of areas that should be considered for representation in the organizational cross-functional workgroup:

- Internet site owners
- Intranet site owners
- Application/web development
- Procurement
- Internal IT
- Communications/marketing
- Sales
- HR
- Legal/civil rights
- Learning
- Project management
- Business controls/compliance office
- Medical/occupational health
- Other?

SCENARIO 5: **THE ACQUISITION**

As part of its overall business strategy, the Acme Corporation, a multinational high-tech software and software services company, is acquiring a smaller company whose technology and products will be integrated into some of Acme's products and its portfolio. The acquisition will give Acme a strong advantage over its competition. As the deal moves forward, Acme consults its team of financial and technology experts to assess the many dimensions of the acquisition, to be certain that the acquired company is all that it's supposed to be and its integration will be smooth and rapid.

Until now, Acme has been fairly diligent about making its strategic products IT accessible and has enjoyed increased revenue worldwide, in both the public and private sectors, as a result. However, the experts consulted about the acquisition failed to include an evaluation of the accessibility of the acquired company's products. With the deal completed, Acme begins executing plans to tightly integrate the acquired technology directly into Acme's key products and begins marketing the smaller company's products under the Acme brand. Only then does someone realize that the acquired products are not accessible. Not only that, but they were built using technologies that were nearly impossible to make accessible without rewriting 90 percent of the acquired code, which would take several years and millions of dollars. Additionally, Acme realizes that its plan to tightly integrate the acquired code into its products would make its now-accessible products inaccessible, putting much of Acme's future revenue at risk.

Too bad that product accessibility wasn't part of the acquisition assessment process, isn't it? Had the accessibility of the acquisition's products been known, Acme could have chosen to back away from the deal or at least could have negotiated a lower price.

CHAPTER 6

COST AND FUNDING MODELS FOR THE IT ACCESSIBILITY INITIATIVE

Like nearly all things worth pursuing, transforming an enterprise for IT accessibility is not easy or inexpensive. Some associated financial costs are obvious, while other elements are not quite as straightforward. Making all elements of your organization IT accessible, while no doubt important, probably isn't the most important aspect of running your business or agency. Therefore, the business's risks and needs must determine the speed and trajectory an IT accessibility transformation initiative should take. For example:

- If an organization concludes that, based on the nature or core of its products and services, IT accessibility is a requirement critical to the market, customers, or community it services, it should launch an aggressive program to bring as many offerings as possible to high levels of compliance as early as possible. This, of course, translates into high front-end startup costs (to be discussed shortly) and ongoing costs in the initial stages of transformation.
- If the business or agency analysis concludes that, for whatever reason, the need for IT accessibility is a high priority but the risks and needs are not urgent, the organization may be

able to spread some initialization and ongoing costs over a longer time frame. But don't let it be too long. Starting too slowly may give the impression that the initiative is less important than the analysis determined, leading to delays in funding and staffing and general lack of focus. Such delays could jeopardize the entire initiative because accomplishing objectives requires a critical mass of IT-accessibility infrastructure.

- Within the organization, the degree of need and risk varies. Some areas or subunits may need accessibility transformation more urgently than others. This is a fairly common scenario, which makes gauging initialization costs a bit more difficult. (In the next section, I will attempt to define some costs that might be considered start-up and those considered ongoing.)

- An organization may decide that top-to-bottom transformation is too much to do at once and will choose to implement a pilot program, selecting one or more subunits for the transformation. Selection could be based on urgency or other relevant factors. Pilot programs, in general, can be useful. However, a word of caution: an accessibility transformation, by definition, requires a majority of its components (I'll be discussing these in later chapters) to be developed and maintained at the organization level to ensure that it meets the needs of the entire organization. Therefore, areas not participating in the pilot will also need to be engaged, or much of what the pilot program accomplishes might have to be significantly redone—at additional expense. The more tactical aspects of accessibility might be more suited to a pilot program, such as compliance testing, integration into a development process, and more—but not the project as a whole.

6.1 START-UP AND ONGOING COSTS

Whether initial or ongoing, costs of accessibility transformation can be broken down to two basic areas:

1. Human resources: the cost of staffing, contracting, managing, and maintaining individuals qualified for or capable of accessibility-related performance at the required levels
2. IT hardware and software: the purchase or development of tools and services used in managing, creating, and testing accessibility

The table that follows provides a summary of the elements of accessibility transformation and their costs, using a relative scale of investment expense for a large organization. Providing actual costs would not be practical or accurate because of the variability of scale, financial practices, and business models within various organizations.

The elements listed should be fairly self-explanatory.

Cost type	Element	Start-up investment level	Ongoing investment level
Human resources	Enterprise/organization staffing	High	Medium
	External consulting	Medium/high	Low/very low
	Subunit/second-level subunit coordinators	Low	Low
	Overall Initiative management	Medium	Low
	Policy and process creation integration	Medium	Low
	Training	Medium	Medium
	Manual testing	Medium	Medium/high
	Management system development	Medium	Low
	Marketing support (private sector)	Medium	Low
IT hardware/ software	Tracking/reporting tools	Medium	Low

Cost type	Element	Start-up investment level	Ongoing investment level
	Enterprise scan tools	Medium	Low
	Enterprise scan tool maintenance	Low	Low
	Developer tools	Medium	Low
	Test tools	Medium	Low
	Development and test tool maintenance	Low	Low
	IT hardware (desktop computers, etc.)	Low	Low
	IT service (database hosting, etc.)	Low	Low

Table 6.1

6.1.1 FUNDING MODELS

Now that you have identified what some key cost elements of accessibility transformation are, you will need to give some thought to how to pay for this initiative. Depending on the organization, this can be straightforward or require more creative solutions.

Most significant accessibility initiatives will require funding on at least two levels: the centralized accessibility area and the subunits.

6.2 CENTRALIZED IT ACCESSIBILITY FUNDING

Most organizations probably already have some centralized functions and conventions for funding them. The first course of action is to understand how existing functions are funded and to try to use that model for adding or integrating funding for centralized accessibility.

This may well be the most effective and efficient approach. That said, it's important to verify that using existing funding models makes sense for the organization and will meet the financial needs of the centralized accessibility project. If existing centralized funding models don't work, you will need to develop a new funding model. In the next section, I discuss some considerations that are important when developing new funding models for centralized IT accessibility.

6.2.1 STRAIGHT ORGANIZATIONAL-LEVEL FUNDING

Top-level funding is an ideal method, no matter where the department is placed on the organizational chart. In most cases, the accessibility department needs such a small piece of the organization's overall budget that top-level funding is reasonably easy to justify—if the business assumptions, projections, and rationale are sound. Considering you've already succeeded in convincing top management that accessibility transformation is necessary, you should encounter little resistance in getting what you need for both initial and ongoing functioning costs as long as the financial projections are reasonably consistent with expectations. It also helps to have members of the company's financial team involved in developing and presenting the funding information, as they speak the language and will be able to explain the details to the other financial staffers and, most importantly, to the folks with the checkbook.

Although most of my experience comes from the private sector, this funding approach should work in the public sector as well. Agencies typically submit and are issued budgets based on requests to a legislative budget board or other similar mechanisms.

6.2.2 SUBUNIT "TAXATION"

Instead of funding the accessibility department as a line item in the budget, private enterprises may decide to "tax" their operating units (usually the ones responsible for profit and loss, which drive funding of enterprise-level operations). "Tax rate" models are based on many factors, including revenue, size, and cost of operations. For the enterprise to determine how much each operating unit should be taxed to fund organization-level functions, it is important to submit and gain approval of a proposed centralized IT-accessibility budget so that it can be included in what is collected in "tax revenues" from the subunits, or "taxpayers." Typically, the subunits will see a breakdown of what their tax is paying for, and the centralized accessibility numbers may show up there, depending on the level of detail in the tax bill. Negotiations about the taxation model often are held to consider tax rates or the amounts or types of services provided to the subunits by the enterprise. If accessibility is included as a line item, especially if it's a new, unfamiliar line item in the tax bill, it may well come under scrutiny. Whatever you do, be prepared, as you may be asked to be fairly specific about what this new centralized function provides and what its associated cost are.

6.2.3 **RESPONSIBILITY FOR CENTRALIZED ACCESSIBILITY FUNDING**

The organization in which centralized accessibility resides is responsible for funding it. Implicit in this approach is that, however, the organization where centralized accessibility resides gets its funding, it and the other functions will negotiate how to carve up the overall operating budget. Accessibility could be relatively unfamiliar to others in the owning organization, which could translate into low priority for funding when having that money is crucial for building and operating centralized accessibility. Having a senior executive of the owning organization to champion accessibility is important to its being funded at the appropriate level. If the owning organization is unable to fund centralized accessibility at the level needed to do the job, methods for supplementing funding exist, and I will discuss them shortly.

6.2.4 **CENTRALIZED ACCESSIBILITY AS A COST CENTER**

Funding centralized accessibility, in whole or in part, by using a cost-center model has merit, but only when most of the start-up activity is complete. The reason is simple. In the initial stages of accessibility transformation, most of the work by the centralized accessibility authority will involve building the infrastructure to support the entire organization, a task not of much interest to cost-center customers. They will be much more interested in technical consulting or having accessibility work performed on their projects; the kinds of activities associated with centralized IT start-up won't be viewed as providing a direct benefit—and won't garner much customer interest in paying for them.

Once much of the start-up work (and one-time costs) is complete and skilled resources are on board, there is a greater potential for a cost-center model because there will be many areas of the organization where skills do not yet exist, such as testing and coding. However, as accessibility matures within the organization, the other subunits will develop their own skilled resources or buy these services from somewhere outside the accessibility cost center, perhaps even from offshore sources. From the perspective of an overall measure of success for IT accessibility at the organization level, it is a clear demonstration of a high level of integration and autonomy in IT accessibility. On the downside, as the subunits become staffed and self-sufficient, such success can affect the centralized accessibility area, which will be dependent on subunit billings to fund significant portions of the organization's IT-accessibility infrastructure.

In theory, the objective is for all subunits to be self-sufficient in making their IT accessible; however, many elements of centralized accessibility serve the entire organization and must remain centralized. Therefore, caution must be exercised when centralized accessibility relies on billings from other areas of the organization to fund its department. Remember, during hard times, budget cuts are a fact of life, and unit and subunit customers may regard accessibility as an optional expense, at least to some degree. When multiple customers across the enterprise face budget cuts, the consequences for accessibility may be fatal.

6.2.5 HYBRID MODELS

A hybrid funding model is a combination of two or more of the funding models described in this chapter. In an ideal world, one funding source would underwrite a substantial amount of the critical mass of resources to ensure that key areas of centralized accessibility can be built and maintained. You may need to secure the remaining funding through direct solicitation of other areas of the organization, either by contracting accessibility work to these areas (similar to the cost-center approach) or by identifying areas of the organization that may require additional services beyond the standard offering provided to all subunits. Some accessibility-related examples might include

- Development of a specific product, service, or tool
- In-depth analysis of a particular product or service tool the subunit is working on or with
- Advanced accessibility-related technical work
- Participation and representation in cross-industry workgroups

Again, care must be exercised in managing this dependency, with realistic, well-conceived contingency plans in place in the event that funding disappears unexpectedly.

6.3 FUNDING SUBUNIT ACCESSIBILITY

Subunit accessibility funding is much more straightforward. With the exception of the subunit and second-level subunit focal points or coordinators, nearly all accessibility-related work will be directly linked to whatever IT projects are being done in those areas.

From the development angle, this will likely translate into additional accessibility training of existing developers or content producers, based on whatever technology platform they are using. In some cases, hiring new people with the requisite expertise may be necessary. The same holds true of accessibility-testing resources. Project schedules may need to be adjusted to account for accessibility-related activities such as manual testing, and schedules may need to allow some additional development time, particularly as developers hone their accessibility skills. Also, project managers will need a relative understanding of accessibility so that they can figure out exactly how to factor IT accessibility activities into project development and test work.

What about funding for unit and subunit focal points and coordinators? Because the number of people in these jobs is usually not that large, there should be many creative ways to cover their headcount. For example, in subunits with many projects, each with its own budget, the coordinator or focal-point costs can be shared by the projects. Depending on the number and size of these projects, the additional charge to each may be minimal. Another option is to fund the coordinators or focal points at the top level of the subunit, while the coordinator resides and is managed lower down.

SCENARIO 6: **THE UPGRADE**

Beth is a highly successful financial analyst for a major brokerage firm. She is a top performer and a mentor to others in the department; they seek out her technical expertise in the use of several large financial applications developed by the firm ten years earlier. Beth is blind but can easily and quickly perform complex tasks within these applications, which are text based and easily accessible.

One day, the company announces that a new, all-encompassing application will be installed the following week to replace the old set of homegrown applications. Hearing this, Beth becomes very concerned about the accessibility of the new application and asks her manager to make inquiries. A few days later, the response comes back: "We contacted the supplier and were told that the application is accessible." Beth is relieved, but once the application is installed, it immediately becomes apparent that it is not accessible. And the old systems are not compatible with the new applications, precluding the possibility of Beth's continuing to use the old systems.

Beth, now extremely upset, contacts the human resources department and requests an accommodation so that she may continue to do her job. Although HR, IT, and other managers explore every avenue, they find that no reasonable accommodation can be made.

Beth's company contacts the product's company numerous times about the gap between its VPAT report and the actual level of accessibility. Her company requests fixes and asks about the accessibility of future product releases. Also, her company reviews the sale contract; company lawyers determine that it makes no mention of accessibility. All avenues exhausted, Beth files a discrimination lawsuit under the Americans with Disabilities Act.

CHAPTER 7

THE STAKEHOLDER ORGANIZATIONS: WHERE IT ACCESSIBILITY PLAYS

As the scenarios and examples throughout this book have demonstrated, IT accessibility comes into play in one form or another in many areas of an organization. Both your accessibility organization and your stakeholder organizations must understand the roles each plays, how IT accessibility should be considered within the stakeholder organizations, and why. In this chapter, I will look at these aspects in depth, providing examples of discrete stakeholder areas that can be found in many large private-sector organizations. In public-sector organizations, some of these stakeholders will not exist. In smaller organizations, some of these areas may be combined or even outsourced. In short, this information should be adapted to suit your organization's specific makeup.

The stakeholders are dependent on the IT accessibility organization to support them in ways necessary to their work. Conversely, as I discussed in chapter 6, IT accessibility organizations may rely on funding from the stakeholders to provide them with meaningful and adequate support in various ways.

7.1 **PRODUCT DEVELOPMENT**

If your organization is in the business of developing IT-related software or hardware for sale as products or services, the product development areas of your business will be among—if not the major—stakeholders for IT accessibility. As I discussed in chapter 3, IT accessibility is important to software and hardware products for reasons of risk mitigation and competitive advantage. Product developers who carefully address IT accessibility can have a direct impact on revenue. Product development teams will need to perform many IT-accessibility activities, and initial and ongoing success will be heavily dependent on expert support from both the centralized accessibility function and the product development team's own accessibility focal points. To fully and successfully integrate IT accessibility into the organization, product development areas will need

- A deep understanding of the current and future technical, regulatory, and market requirements for IT accessibility that are relevant to the marketplaces served by the enterprise
- General and specific IT accessibility training for developers, testers, and other professionals in product development
- Technical guidance and consulting by accessibility experts during development (at least initially)
- Integration of accessibility criteria into the organization's product-related business processes and development lifecycles
- Accessibility evaluations of competitors' products or services, when feasible
- Creation of accurate accessibility documentation (VPATs or other documentation) during development and product release cycles
- Integration of accessibility feature descriptions into marketing and sales material
- Procurement or creation of developer/test tools to facilitate IT accessibility

- Procurement of accessible software or contracted software services that will be integrated into your organization's products
- Development of product-line or brand-level accessibility plans and strategies

Because the centralized accessibility organization may use a funding model that includes securing financial support from stakeholders, funding from the product-development areas may be more substantial than from other stakeholders.

7.2 THE INTERNAL IT ORGANIZATION

The internal IT organization will probably be the most complex area with regard to the integration of accessibility, and it will increase in complexity as the overall organization grows and becomes more diversified. Although the internal IT organization is not selling products or services to the marketplace, it requires many of the same IT-accessibility services as the product-development area but with additional considerations. Just think about the range and diversity of the IT used to run an organization. End-user desktop products like word-processing, spreadsheet, and presentation software; server-based email and collaboration software; intranet applications; operating systems; databases; business-management and web content-management packages; manufacturing and logistics IT systems—there may be hundreds, even thousands, of such applications for very large, diversified, multinational organizations. When I worked at IBM, for example, it had thousands of applications running in its IT environment worldwide on any given day, with hundreds of new applications being deployed and retired annually. At that time, the number of individuals involved in developing and maintaining this huge environment was in the tens of thousands worldwide. While you might consider IBM to be a somewhat extreme example, it may not be as extreme as you think. Many large enterprises have internal IT environments on the scale of IBM's.

Also, unless your organization's work and mission are so specialized that everything used by your employees is custom developed by your internal IT organization (a near impossibility), vendors will supply much of the IT hardware, software, and services used internally. This means that accessibility will need to be considered in every aspect of the procurement process. I will cover this in greater detail in chapter 8.

The bottom line? The internal IT organization will need a lot of help. But making everything compliant with accessibility needs, standards, regulations, and policies should be viewed as a relative objective, given that most of the IT an organization purchases will range in accessibility compliance from very poor to very good. The internally developed IT will also be problematic because many of the homegrown applications being used have already been written and deployed; it may be difficult, impractical, or expensive to retrofit these for accessibility. Going forward, however, the development of new in-house applications will provide excellent opportunities for building accessible applications. Therefore, a plan of attack for internal accessibility will need to be devised; it should include analysis and recommendations from the centralized accessibility organization.

In addition to all the elements listed in section 7.1, stakeholders will need to consult accessibility experts about procuring IT software and hardware and prioritizing what to work on and when.

7.3 WEB COMMERCE AND COMMUNICATIONS

Are you wondering why the organization's website isn't considered part of the internal IT environment? Well, it is and it isn't. While the infrastructure for the external web is probably hosted and maintained by the internal IT organization, it's the marketing and communications areas that most likely have control over the content, look, and feel of the website. Developers and content producers won't be the only folks involved in building your websites; this will also be done by "creatives," who will be obsessed with providing the richest experience possible, using the latest web technologies to bring the web presence to life. However, this approach may render a website highly inaccessible, unless your enterprise makes accessibility a top priority in the design of the site. Website inaccessibility carries a high degree of exposure, as the examples in chapter 3 demonstrate, so striving for a rich experience for everyone is important.

This is particularly true in the case of web commerce. The task of buying a product over the Internet may seem simple enough, at least for a sighted individual, but what about consumers who rely on screen readers to "see" products to decide what to buy? In many situations today, making a purchase might entail navigating away from your website to a transaction-processing site outside your Internet domain. Are the sites your organization uses accessible? Can a consumer with a disability successfully complete the transaction and with the degree of ease enjoyed by someone who does not have a disability?

7.4 PROCUREMENT

Although it may never have occurred to you that procurement is the granddaddy of IT accessibility, it is. In fact, the first IT accessibility regulation—US Section 508—is a procurement regulation. Section 508 was created to ensure that IT products purchased by the federal government are accessible and comply with a specific set of criteria. Given this somewhat lengthy history of accessibility in procurement, you'd think it would be well understood—and well-integrated into the procurement processes and culture for IT-related purchases.

However, even at the writing of this second edition, procuring accessible IT hardware, software, products, and services remains challenging. For one thing, IT procurement can be complicated in and of itself, let alone with the introduction of IT accessibility requirements, The process can involve a lot of steps with requirements and technical specifications provided by experts, as well as from the procurement area itself, which has many duties, such as writing and reviewing the solicitations, searching for suppliers' products and services, analyzing the bids, writing the contracts and conditions, and validating that the supplier meets the conditions of the contracts. Accessibility has to be considered and integrated into nearly every step in the procurement process for IT-related purchases. The talents of skilled IT accessibility experts will be needed to

- Integrate IT accessibility into the requirements
- Develop accessibility language for bid solicitations and contracts
- Review and analyze supplier bid responses related to accessibility requirements
- Review and understand vendor validation results accessibility testing
- Make go-no go accessibility recommendations on proceeding with the procurement based on risk levels

From an overall IT-procurement perspective, the accessibility experts will also need to integrate all these steps and more into the organization's procurement processes to ensure that accessibility can never be left out—unless done so intentionally.

7.5 **HUMAN RESOURCES**

Because the HR department of an organization is typically responsible for all aspects of an employee's tenure with the enterprise, one can see how important IT accessibility can be and how risky the lack of accessible IT can be. Recall some of the examples and scenarios provided in earlier chapters. For an organization's own employees, HR is where the rubber meets the road with regard to IT accessibility.

Here are some examples of events in the employee "life cycle":

- Recruitment, hiring, and orientation
- Training and career development
- IT-based job duties and responsibilities
- Personal information tools (salary, retirement planning, timekeeping, medical benefits, and the like)

- Performance-evaluation tools
- Post-retirement tools (pension, investment tracking, etc.)

IT pervades every aspect of an employee's working life and beyond. Therefore, to have an inclusive organization, IT systems or applications touched by employees need to be made accessible, including the tools and systems that HR personnel use to process and manage the business side of HR.

Given the number of HR systems used by employees from all areas of the organization, the internal IT organization and HR must have a strong relationship. This relationship may even be described as a dependency, because the IT department would be responsible for developing, procuring, or contracting IT for one of its biggest customers, the HR organization. And because all employees are required in some way or another to interact with IT personnel systems, noncompliance can pose great risks to the enterprise. Therefore, HR management needs to be diligent about ensuring the accessibility of all tools and applications that employees use, because if problems arise, you can be sure that HR will be involved. This might even include an HR sign off as part of the procurement or deployment of internal IT.

7.6 ADVERTISING, MARKETING COMMUNICATIONS, AND MEDIA

Up until the early to mid-2000s, advertising and marketing materials came in two formats: print and video. Today, in the digital age, many new and innovative channels have emerged that offer tremendous benefits, and, in many cases, advantages, over traditional media.

Every day, electronic information reaches current and potential customers directly and indirectly, using such diverse methods as email advertising and promotional offers, highly targeted search results pages, to huge, diverse websites, ads on nearly every web page that take you right to the website of the advertiser, and clever new applications of social media. When any of these new channels fail to provide access for consumers with disabilities, the result may be not only lost revenue but litigation as well.

Even a simple, direct email can lead to lost sales or litigation or both if it contains inaccessible content. Have you ever received an email offer from a reputable company that seems to contain nothing until you click the "show picture" button? Then a beautiful colorful graphic appears with all the information that you need to know about the offer, product, and special pricing. Is it accessible? Does it include a means to provide the same information to a blind user? If not, did the advertiser neglect this intentionally? Probably not. The advertiser probably just did not know about accessibility or had not established an in-house mechanism for catching such oversights.

Has your organization posted a video without captions on a social media page or site? Or has it paid for a graphical link from a news page on which it advertises that takes the potential customer right to your organization's international, inaccessible website? Such simple lapses can have potentially profound consequences. Making sure that your organization's websites, advertising, and marketing communications and media are accessible will require support in lots of ways from your accessibility organization.

7.7 INTERNAL COMMUNICATIONS

In the modern world, electronic information distribution is the standard mechanism for communicating to internal staff. Therefore, all forms of internal communications must be usable by employees with disabilities.

Examples of such communications include the following:

- Email (text only or otherwise)
- Documents: technical, personnel information, electronic forms, and the like
- Videos

- Webcasts
- Podcasts
- Social networks
- Communications-specific web pages

Because your intranet may be a key delivery vehicle for internal information, the internal IT organization has a responsibility to provide the infrastructure, content management systems, and other services that support internal communications through that intranet. If employees can post to the intranet without appropriate governance/management rules, you can add accessibility issues to your other content-management challenges.

7.8 EDUCATION- AND TECHNOLOGY-BASED LEARNING

From the first day of employment and throughout an employee's tenure, education and training are a vital part of any organization's staff-development plan. Technical training, management training, required training, and general skills training curricula are available to your organization's employees and staff. Internal education and training can take many forms:

- Instructor-led classroom training
- Online or desktop tutorials
- Webinars
- Telephone- or PC-based calls
- Video (live or recorded)

In today's world, most of these (even those led by instructors) will be delivered, in part or entirely, by means of IT technology. Courses themselves must be IT accessible. Therefore, the content producers or editors need to ensure that the correct IT-accessibility criteria are integrated into the content of each type of training. This means that they will need to be trained to produce accessible courses and other content. Also keep in mind that many organizations purchase training and education materials or contract for training personnel from third-party suppliers and that the training may be held at a physical location or through a website external to your organization. When this occurs, your procurement organization will be playing a role, as will the internal IT area for training that is delivered via your organization's intranet.

One more area of consideration for IT-based internal training will be the learning management system (LMS) itself, which would contain online course catalogs, course descriptions, enrollment forms, and the delivery framework. The LMS will also need to be IT accessible, whether it is developed internally or purchased.

It goes without saying that if you are in the business of creating and providing either off-the-shelf or customized training to both public- and private-sector organizations, accessibility is important to your customers and to the bottom line.

7.9 LEGAL DEPARTMENT

While the legal department of an organization is an important stakeholder, it may not be dealing with accessibility issues on a day-to-day basis; however, when a significant IT accessibility issue arises, in-house lawyers will play a leading role in bringing about a resolution. IT accessibility issues can be complicated, which means that the legal team will need a solid grasp of IT accessibility in the following areas:

- Laws and regulations relevant to accessibility (the Americans with Disabilities Act, US Section 508, the British Disabilities Discrimination Act, and specific laws of other countries or jurisdictions)
- Documentation for accessibility compliance
- Precedents and cases pending involving IT accessibility law

The legal team will in some cases be dependent on the organization's centralized IT accessibility team for current and complete information in these areas, in addition to whatever the specific issues are on the table at the time. What might these issues be? Here are a few general examples of issues that may require the attention of a lawyer:

- Disputes between the organization and its customers related to the organization's products' not meeting accessibility levels documented in the products' VPATs or other reporting documents
- Disputes between the organization and its suppliers related to the IT accessibility of purchased IT products or components
- Disputes between the organization and the public or its customers related to any failure of the organization's informational, commercial, or entertainment websites to meet accessibility levels required by law
- Disputes between the organization and employees resulting from inaccessibility of internal IT that prevents employees from performing key aspects of their job or that denies them access to organizational or personal information they need

It also important to realize that whenever an issue arises, it could quickly devolve into a class-action suit. Therefore, it is important for management and the human relations department to err on the side of caution by engaging the legal team as early as possible and ensuring that the team thoughtfully reviews potential solutions.

In the public sector, an organization may also have a civil rights department. If separate from the general legal team, the civil rights team should also be engaged through the life of the issue.

7.10 BUSINESS CONTROLS OR COMPLIANCE OFFICE

I consider the compliance office one of the big sticks that can be used to help areas of an organization better understand the need for IT accessibility when not completely sold on the idea. However, asking business control and compliance teams to perform an accessibility audit on a troublesome area is does not promote partnership, cooperation, and teamwork. Using this approach is a last resort.

There may be other reasons to seek an IT accessibility audit. Here are a few examples:

- IT accessibility is an important, relatively new area with many ramifications for the organization, and management wants to ensure that implementation is proceeding correctly.
- An audit is part of the remedy for a significant accessibility issue (that is, one that has given rise to a lawsuit or is about to).
- An accessibility audit is one of many routine compliance audits that the organization regularly undergoes.

If you work in or manage the centralized accessibility organization, the business controls or compliance office can be a valuable ally in accomplishing IT accessibility objectives, albeit in a heavy-handed way. Like most auditing bodies, business controls and compliance have far-reaching authority, can delve as deeply as necessary into any area of your organization, and can produce a final assessment that results in actions that affect almost any aspect of an organization, including the following:

- Process changes
- QA integration
- Modification of project plans, budgets, and revenue projections
- Personnel changes in management

Most areas of an organization shudder when they learn that the business controls or compliance office will be auditing their area. Immediately the departments will begin a self-assessment and try to correct the problems identified in an attempt to mitigate them before the auditors find them.

On the other hand, the centralized accessibility area will view such an audit as positive because it forces other departments to deal with accessibility in accordance with the overall organization's accessibility policy and governance requirements.

However, business controls and compliance auditors can do their job effectively only if they have a thorough understanding of accessibility, the associated organizational policies, and the business processes in which accessibility must be integrated. Educating the auditors in these areas is the responsibility of the centralized accessibility area.

7.11 **MEDICAL OR OCCUPATIONAL HEALTH**

Although medical or occupational health personnel may not be direct players in IT accessibility, they may need some support from the accessibility organization in working with specific individual employees. The accessibility team may be called upon to perform the following:

- Evaluate the merits of tools or assistive technologies that may help resolve IT accessibility challenges for individual employees
- Evaluate the interoperability of candidate tools or assistive technologies with the hardware and software that an individual employee needs to perform her or his job and access IT resources
- Develop accommodations for specific individuals when accessibility can not be accomplished in mainstream ways.

SCENARIO 7: **INACCURATE ACCESSIBILITY DOCUMENTATION**

Companies A, B, and C are competing for a large, complex government IT contract. Each company's bid includes a combination of multiple software products that comprise a whole solution. Accessibility is a key element of the contract, and VPAT documentation is required. Companies A and B understand accessibility well and do a good job of accurately documenting the compliance levels of the products in their solutions. In fact, they even do their own testing of components that are from third-party suppliers. While not everything in their offerings is 100 percent accessible, the problem areas are accurately documented in the final bid.

Accessibility is a new area for Company C, whose skills and experience in that area are much lower than its competitors'. Partly because of lack of knowledge, and partly because of its aggressive effort to win the bid, its accessibility documentation does not reflect the actual accessibility levels of the products in its bid. No testing is performed on third-party products to confirm their documentation, which is also inaccurate.

Company C wins the bid because the documentation shows its accessibility is the best of the three bidders'. The contract, which includes IT accessibility clauses, is signed, and the solution installed. Shortly thereafter, the government agency finds severe accessibility issues and demands, per the contract, that they be corrected within thirty days. The company cannot meet this requirement because its staff does not have the requisite accessibility skills and because its solution used inaccessible third-party products that they do not control.

The government assesses financial penalties until the problems are corrected and eventually sues Company C, claiming it falsified its bid documentation and breached the contract.

CHAPTER 8

THE FOCUS AREAS

In chapter 7, I discussed the stakeholders and how accessibility plays a role in their operations. In this chapter, I will delve into the mechanics of what needs to be done in key areas of IT accessibility transformation.

8.1 GOVERNANCE AND OVERSIGHT, PROCEDURES, AND DOCUMENTATION

As I discussed in chapter 4, the development of an IT accessibility policy is the fundamental action that will drive nearly every aspect of your organization's IT accessibility initiative. Although the centralized accessibility function is not necessarily responsible for doing all the work required to make all the organization's IT accessible, it should, if chartered correctly, have a level of accountability for the total initiative for the organization. This responsibility should not be viewed as something in name only. The activities and services that the centralized accessibility area provides are the primary implementation vehicle for making IT accessible in all areas of the organization. While the centralized organization may not have ownership of IT accessibility at unit, subunit, or product level, it provides overall management, business and technical guidance, and supporting infrastructure critical to the progress and success of the organization's IT accessibility initiative.

Therefore, the early part of this chapter is largely devoted to the mission, work, and actions of the organization-wide accessibility function, all of which flow from and support the organization's IT accessibility policy.

8.1.1 GUIDANCE DOCUMENTATION

Let's say the IT accessibility policy is written, reviewed, approved, and published in the appropriate place in your organization, where other policy documents are retained. Now what? The next step is to develop or provide detailed operational information in support of that policy. Included should be IT accessibility information that is relevant or applicable to the entire organization and its operating units and subunits, providing information, instructions, and technical guidance on how and where to implement IT accessibility in support of the organization's accessibility policy.

This information needs to be readily available to every employee of the organization, as it will be the primary source of information about IT accessibility. An intranet website or information portal devoted to accessibility makes an excellent centralized repository for this purpose. (Be sure it's accessible!) Bear in mind that the accessibility coordinators or focal points for those organizational units and subunits may also choose to develop and maintain their own repositories (websites, etc.) with accessibility information specific to their area. As this occurs, these secondary websites tend to take information from the centralized location and republish it on their unit or subunit accessibility pages. This practice should be discouraged, as it creates information-synchronization problems, which can lead to inconsistent information and confusion. The solution is to have pointers or links to the main organization's accessibility repository.

8.1.2 **GUIDANCE DOCUMENTATION CONTENT**

Now that you have established a place to hold all the policy support information and deliver it to all employees, what should it include?

8.1.2.1 **DEVELOPER GUIDES AND SUPPORT**

The developer guides and support section should provide relevant technical information for creating accessible products, websites, web content documents, and more. If this section were a paper reference book, its pages would be frayed and dirty from overuse.

The technical requirements specified by whichever standards and regulations your organization has chosen to follow are the most important information in this section. That information should include the following:

- The accessibility specifications that must be met
- The rationale for each specification
- Code examples and techniques for meeting the requirements of various development platforms used in your organization
- Checklists of accessibility requirements for developers to use to confirm that they have addressed all specifications and guidelines
- Accessibility testing requirements, procedures, and materials, including
- Methodologies
- Test case examples
- Techniques
- Development/testing tools
- Links to external, industry-recognized resources for developers and testers, including links to official websites that detail the standards, regulations, or guidelines that your organization has committed to meet

8.1.2.2 **THE ORGANIZATION'S ACCESSIBILITY POLICY, SCOPE, AND APPLICABILITY**

The operational aspects of IT accessibility for the organization need their own section, which should include guidance and governance information that defines the hows, whys, and wheres of your organization's IT accessibility program:

- The official accessibility policy document
- Definitions and details of the organizational areas, functions, programs, and other areas where IT accessibility compliance applies (such as stakeholder areas; see chapter 7). These should not be specific to products or types of products, since excluding one or several can be an invitation to find a way to ignore the mandate for IT accessibility. General phrasing such as "all Internet content and applications" is broad and nonspecific, making it difficult to get around the policy.
- The management system for the IT accessibility program, including the following:
  o A high-level description of the governance model
  o Roles and responsibilities for IT accessibility of staff in various positions within the organization
  o The role of IT accessibility in product development and business processes and procedures, including detailed information about how and where accessibility is to be integrated, including links to the business and development processes and procedures whose IT is to be made accessible
  o Procedures for dealing with noncompliance, exceptions, or variances
  o Information about how to develop VPATs (if applicable) or other IT accessibility documentation
  o Other documents or links to related policies, regulations, or standards

8.1.2.3 **IT ACCESSIBILITY IN PROCUREMENT**

IP accessibility in procurement is a particularly thorny area. Nearly every organization, whether in the public or private sector, purchases a tremendous amount of IT from third-party suppliers and uses it into nearly every area aspect of its business, or mission. Procurement touches so many areas of the organization, procurement of IT warrants dedicated space in the repository but also warrants its own section (8.4) in this revised edition of the book. The procurement section of the repository might include the following topics:

- Specific policy documents for procuring accessible IT
- Detailed IT procurement instructions or process flows with accessibility criteria and actions included
- Online or classroom training for contracts and procurement professionals
- Boilerplate language approved by the organization and for use as applicable to specify IT accessibility when soliciting bids and negotiating contracts. Accessibility compliance information (such as VPATs) for existing contracts and products.

8.1.2.4 OTHER DOCUMENTATION

Your enterprise may choose to include other information based on the nature of its business or organization. Here's a good rule of thumb: include any information that can assist your organization's stakeholders and employees in making its products or internal IT accessible.

8.1.3 PROCESS INTEGRATION

Given that IT accessibility is important in so many areas of your organization, how do you ensure that accessibility criteria are implemented consistently and professionally? While having an IT accessibility policy and lots of supporting information is a step in the right direction, the most effective strategy is to tightly integrate IT accessibility into the relevant business and development processes that are already in use within your organization.

8.1.3.1 **FACTORS TO CONSIDER WHEN INTEGRATING ACCESSIBILITY INTO PROCESSES**

1. Is the candidate process the correct process to integrate IT accessibility? Is it logical and relevant? Is it a process that employees actually use? If the answer to any of these questions is no, find another process that accomplishes the same thing where the answers are "yes." Every enterprise has developed processes to solve particular problems in the past. Such processes may have become obsolete or less important over the years. One way to ensure you select the correct process for IT integration is to work with key personnel within that organization to review their processes for the best fit. If no relevant process exists that makes sense, you may need to develop one.

2. Where in a process do the potential points for integrating IT accessibility lie? Business and development processes can have many steps and phases, so a good understanding of the process and IT accessibility is critical to determining the integration points. It is a safe assumption that a development process will have many integration points, whereas other, less complex business processes may have fewer points of integration.

   The example that follows uses an analysis of a very large business/development process and shows the potential points of integration for IT accessibility. In this example, the only place where IT accessibility criteria was originally placed was in the "Test" subprocess, although after a thorough analysis, the company needed to consider making its IT accessible everywhere a small triangle appears.

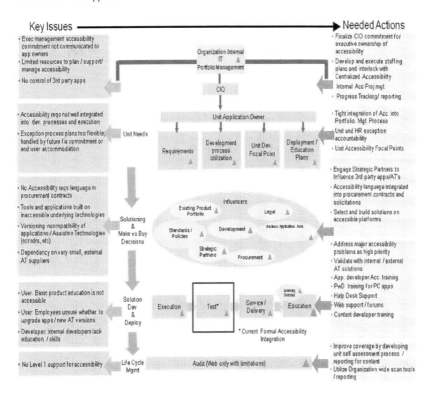

Current Internal App Processes / Recommended Actions   ▲ = Accessibility Criteria Integration points

Fig. 4. Example of an IT accessibility process analysis

3. The IT accessibility integration criteria (actions, procedures, subprocesses, etc.). The preceding graphic depicts the analysis of a very large business area, its major components, and points where the company determined it needed accessibility. Each block identified with a triangle has its own process or set of processes. The next step is to understand what these processes are and do, and to integrate specific IT accessibility–related tasks and procedures into those processes. Most software-development and web-management processes contain steps and procedures for quality and corrective actions. These processes usually have systematic ways of addressing, tracking, and fixing problems that have been identified

(often referred to as defects), and integrating IT accessibility criteria there is a crucial step. Without integration there, the likelihood of fixing problems will be slim. The following graphic is another example of IT accessibility integration, this time into an IT procurement process.

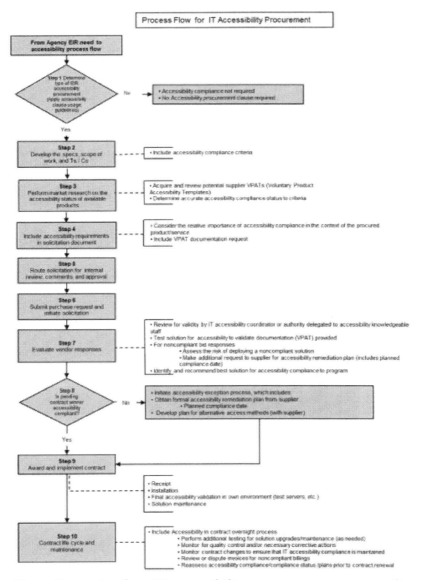

Fig. 5. Example of an IT accessibility procurement process flow

4. Your review of the revised process proposal with stakeholders and their concurrence with the revisions. Changing processes to include IT accessibility steps can affect projects and entire departments. It may add steps, time, and labor, so it's important that the process users and stakeholders understand and agree with the proposed changes. In obtaining their concurrence, try to anticipate and be prepared to address stakeholder questions or concerns, and keep an open mind when stakeholders make suggestions for modification. There is, however, a "tipping point" at which the stakeholder's suggestions or desires could make the integration much less effective. Recognize that the amount of compromise can affect the overall effectiveness of the process changes and the success of the IT accessibility program.

5. Assuming that the stakeholders give the go-ahead, the next step is to develop implementation plans. The plans should contain the following:

   • The effective date when the process changes go into effect; this should be far enough in the future to provide time for appropriate preparatory activities.
   • Key activities in support of meeting the deadline.
   • A planned communication that includes changes and reasons for them.
   • A list of prerequisites for implementation (such as technical training).
   • Officially publishing the changes to the existing process documentation.
   • A plan for addressing questions as the new process is implemented.

Initially, users of a revised process may have a lot of questions, even if training is part of the pre-implementation plans and activities. You will need to ensure that adequate support resources are available, although they can be decreased over time. Also, once implemented, you may find that some process changes don't work quite as well as they did on paper, so be prepared to adjust or change the process to make it as effective and useful as possible.

8.1.4 **IT ACCESSIBILITY EXCEPTIONS**

Even after IT accessibility has been integrated throughout the organization, some products, websites, documents, will no doubt, remain inaccessible for one reason or another. Such items will be considered exceptions to policy compliance. Therefore, the centralized accessibility function and subunits need a process for documenting and managing these exceptions. As you may recall, the content of the IT accessibility policy should contain language for governing exceptions, but the criteria and processes for handling exceptions will need to be defined. Perhaps a single process can handle all exceptions across the organization, or the organization may need multiple exceptions processes tailored for specific areas. The exceptions process and documentation should include information about the IT unit that requires the exception. Here are some examples of key information to include in the exceptions documentation:

- Name of the IT
- Name of the IT owner (a product manager, a team lead, a project manager, etc.)
- Release date
- IT description (purpose, audience, number of users, etc.)
- Justification for requiring an exception (cost, technology limitations, no available accessible products in marketplace, risks, etc.)
- Risk assessment of releasing inaccessible IT
- Planned date for accessibility
- Alternate methods of access (e.g., 24/7 phone support)
- Recommendation for approval by the accessibility coordinator of the area to which the IT belongs
- Signature of the executive owner of the IT (head of the unit or subunit)

Once the exception has gone through the process and been approved by the executive owner of the IT, the document or record should be located in a centralized repository so it can easily be accessed by those in need of such information, such as auditors.

8.1.5 **BUSINESS CONTROLS AND AUDITS**

Once the IT accessibility integration process is completed, which of the following is an acceptable way that can you verify that new processes are actually being followed?

1. Wait for the first products or websites developed after the effective date to launch and test them for accessibility.
2. Politely ask stakeholders whether they followed the new process and whether their deliverables are accessible (self-audit).
3. Integrate IT accessibility into the organization's business controls processes as a compliance policy, and train the business controls organization how to audit the stakeholder organizations to ensure that they have done everything they were supposed to do.

In case you were unsure, the third strategy is the correct one.

Accessibility governance is tricky. If it's soft peddled, as in methods 1 and 2, the transformation journey may take a long time or fail completely. If governance is too heavy-handed, many folks will be upset, which may result in slow or even unsuccessful adoption. Therefore you need a good balance of carrot and stick, and what that balance is will vary from area to area within your organization. Asking units or subunits of organizations to self-report is an example of a carrot approach. It gives each area a sense of ownership and responsibility. Where this approach falls short is in the timely collection of the data and the quality of the information being self reported which can often be "overly optimistic," a polite way to say inaccurate, which is a classic problem of self-auditing and self-reporting. To ensure accuracy and timeliness, the organization should consider collecting stakeholder information itself through various methods and tools.

8.1.5.1 AUTOMATED ACCESSIBILITY WEB SCANNING

Organization-wide, centralized, automated accessibility web scanning is a good example of a combined approach to gauging compliance. An automated web scanning tool can crawl the organization's internet and intranet pages, looking for and reporting accessibility errors. The pages and web applications are out there, live and available to the scan tool, so no one has to put aside regular work to collect the information. It's collected quietly and accurately. The scans should be done at some regular calendar interval, and the planned scan dates should be communicated a week or two before the scan starts. This allows the areas to have a look themselves and fix what they can before the scans. Keep in mind, however, that scan tools have limitations and are capable of checking only for a subset of accessibility criteria (about 1/3) and are not a substitute for manual testing. Most scans do an excellent job of finding the accessibility errors they are can discover, and the results can provide a good indication of how much effort is going into website/web applications accessibility.

8.1.5.2 MANUAL DATABASE

Automated scan tools for non-web IT don't really exist, so in this case, manual testing will need to be performed and the results documented. Instead of having each area maintain its own records of this activity, a centralized database should be set up to contain the results from all areas of the organization. The database should be owned by the centralized accessibility function, but the testing and resulting data would be entered in the database and owned by the stakeholder areas. If the database is structured correctly and allows for the generation of progress reports and their delivery to organization leaders, it can be an effective tool to help drive progress.

8.1.5.3 **IT ACCESSIBILITY AUDITS**

The audit approach uses auditors from the area that oversees your organization's compliance programs to examine IT accessibility from start to finish. This involves the following:

- Confirmation that the appropriate processes for IT accessibility are in place
- Confirmation that IT accessibility is being performed according to the processes used
- Evaluation of deliverables' accessibility
- Identification of corrective actions needed
- Documentation and reporting of findings to the appropriate organizational managers.

As I mentioned in chapter 7, auditors will require some level of training in IT accessibility to know what to look for. Audits can be conducted on a regular schedule, randomly performed, or done at the request of a concerned party. In the interests of impartiality and maintaining a good working relationship with the staff in the centralized accessibility area, the audits should be performed without direct assistance from the centralized IT accessibility team. However, asking the centralized IT accessibility team to review the findings and recommendations of the audit would be both valuable and appropriate.

8.1.6 **ESTABLISHING METRICS AND TRACKING PROGRESS**

With IT accessibility integrated into the appropriate processes within your organization, it's time to think about how to measure progress and the overall success of your accessibility initiative. Finding the appropriate aspects of your program to measure can be a bit challenging, particularly at the beginning of the journey.

8.1.6.1 **DEVELOPING GOALS**

Of course, it's easy for someone to stand up and make a statement like, "We want all of our organization's internal IT and product

IT to be 100 percent accessible by X date." However, such a goal, while noble, is not realistic given the complexity of the project. Achieving perfect accessibility across an entire organization should be considered a theoretical target, at least for the foreseeable future. Of course, the policy your organization develops should support perfect implementation, but the cost and technology needed to achieve this goal would probably break the bank. Developing short-term and long-term goals based on an accessibility strategy, and the priorities contained within it, is a much more meaningful and realistic approach.

8.1.6.2 SHORT-TERM GOALS

At the beginning of your organization's accessibility initiative, setting short-term goals is important and can be both strategic and tactical. Short-term goals may be indirectly related to making IT accessible. Here are some examples:

- Completion of general accessibility awareness training by 50 percent of staff within eight months, and 100 percent within sixteen months
- Completion of accessibility training by all Java programmers within six months
- Establishment of a baseline of accessibility for the organization's external website
- Exploration and selection of web scan tools for regular scanning of internal and external websites
- Appointment of accessibility focal points for all necessary units and subunits

All these examples are certainly related to making IT accessible, but they are more related to enablement than execution. They are short term activities with long-term impact. Progress can be easily tracked and measured by using metrics such as deadlines for completion.

8.1.6.3 **LONG-TERM GOALS**

Most long-term goals should be related to measuring actual progress in making your organization's IT accessible. These won't be "checkbox" items, as long-term goals will need to be established and probably agreed upon by the various stakeholders to ensure consensus. The goals for various stakeholder organizations may be customized based on the nature of their work, but the common elements are establishing these goals, measuring the progress toward meeting them over time, and reporting the results at regular intervals (e.g., quarterly). Here are some examples of metrics for long-range accessibility goals:

- Percentage of Internet pages with accessibility errors
- Percentage of intranet pages with accessibility errors
- Percentage of procured IT products and services for internal use that are accessible
- Number of exceptions created
- Total number of compliant/noncompliant products in the IT portfolio
- Number of recently announced compliant and noncompliant products and services

Remember, events may occur within your organization that can skew your long-term tracking data. These need to be accounted for before, during, or after they occur. For example, your organization is a commercial enterprise that, for strategic purposes, chooses to acquire another company or bases its business plan on acquiring companies. The compliance levels of the acquired companies' portfolios will certainly have an effect on the data your organization uses to track accessibility progress once the acquisitions are folded in. Because of this, your organization may need a method factoring the acquisition strategy into the overall data that doesn't skew the measurements' results for the entire organization. This isn't all that difficult, as the acquisitions can simply be tracked separately and given a grace period until they are counted in the main progress reports. That way, they don't counteract all the hard work being done in the areas where high compliance levels have been achieved.

When an organization purchases components for IT it is developing, and those components reduce the level of compliance upon integration, the situation can get more complicated. Accounting for scenarios like this takes foresight. Figuring out how to track such occurrences should be the least of your organization's worries. Rather, you should be focused on the effects and risks resulting from such integration. (Hint: Proper integration of IT accessibility processes and procedures into an organization's acquisition, development, and procurement processes can help ensure that accessibility levels of the acquired companies' products or components are known and considered before the deals are completed.)

8.1.7 REPORTING PROGRESS

Now that your organization has established the metrics and begun tracking progress, here are a few fundamental elements to consider when developing your reporting plan:

- Who should receive the reports?
- How often should reports be published?
- What information should they contain?
- How can they best be used to drive progress?

8.1.7.1 AUDIENCE FOR REPORT DATA

If your organization does a good job of developing the goals and defining an appropriate set of metrics, it will produce great data. However, all the data in the world may not help your organization unless it can be effectively used to drive the progress and trajectory of the accessibility transformation. The best way to ensure that the data can be used effectively is to get it into the hands of the people within your organization who can look at the results and take actions necessary to keep progress on track. The primary audience for progress reporting should be at the executive levels of the organization. These individuals are most capable of seeing the whole picture of the organization that they manage, without a lot of bias (positive or negative) toward any particular area. They are used to looking at high-level reports and will most likely know how to use them to facilitate any actions that the results suggest.

It might also be appropriate, depending on your organization, to provide the reports to managers one or two levels down from the executives, so that they are aware of where things stand and can explain in detail any results that the executives may want to know more about. From there, reports can trickle down as deemed appropriate or useful.

Organizationally, it makes sense to provide a report to at least one person from every stakeholder organization so that stakeholders are kept abreast of progress and can anticipate how the results might affect their organization.

8.1.7.2 FREQUENCY OF REPORT PUBLISHING

Frequency of reporting is a delicate balance to strike. If reports are published infrequently, there will long intervals between actions taken based on the data and the next report. If they are published too often, there may be little change between reports, and people will start to ignore them. Four to six times a year would be what I consider acceptable frequency for official report publishing. Depending on progress (or lack thereof) or other factors, the interval can always be adjusted.

8.1.7.3 REPORT CONTENT

A good rule of thumb for reporting IT accessibility progress is that high-level audiences require high-level reports. Like any executive-level report, an accessibility report should be concise and powerful.

It should contain the following:

- Executive summaries of results

- Graphics that summarize the data based on the established metrics
- Highlights of any significant accomplishments or effects that occurred during the reporting period (new acquisitions, significant compliance gains, external factors, etc.)
- Planned or recommended actions needed for continued progress, or issues or roadblocks that need removal
- Detailed background information so that when the report reaches operational managers, they will be able to access additional reference material on a particular product or area

Depending on the size and structure of your organization, you may choose to create and distribute multiple reports, customized for specific areas of the organization. For example, it may not make sense to include the reports for an organization's internal IT accessibility compliance in an executive report going to development or brand executives. The organization's structure and other factors will determine the best approach. Following are some examples of report

Executive Summary Data

Assessment	YE 2009	2Q10	3Q2010	% QTQ Chg
Total Compliance	62%	73%	72%	-1
- Current Product Portfolio	60%	70%	63%	-7
- Products under development	63%	74%	74%	0

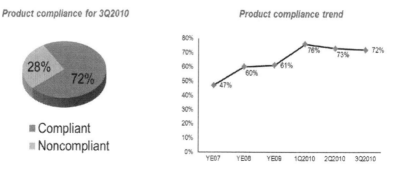

Fig. 6. Example of an IT accessibility executive report summary

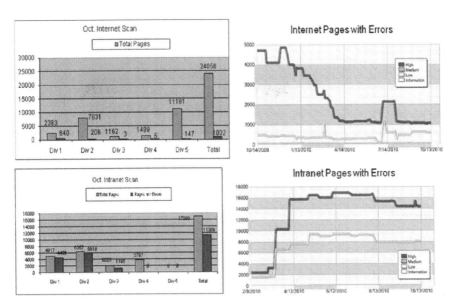

Fig. 7. Example of an IT accessibility automated scan report

8.1.7.4 **OTHER CONSIDERATIONS**

Assuming that the accessibility information database and input process are set up correctly, the report data should be easy to extract from the database information. It's important to recall that while the main organizational level maintains the database and selects and uses the tracking tools, the stakeholder areas provide and maintain the data. In the interest of collaboration, it's always a good idea for the database owners to notify the stakeholders a couple of weeks before data is extracted for reports. This allows stakeholders to ensure that their data is current at the time of the data extraction. Also, in the interest of collaboration, it's a good idea to share the results with the stakeholders and allow them to provide comments, action plans, and the like that can be included in the finished reports. That said, a bit of diplomacy needs to be exercised during this process, as a stakeholder organization may not be happy with its results and may want to use its review as an opportunity to downplay (or even try to remove) issues or problems that need to be addressed. Politics!

8.1.8 **DRIVING PROGRESS WITH REPORT DATA**

Documenting and reporting on accessibility progress requires a bit of effort by stakeholders and those responsible for overseeing the governance of the initiative. Creating and sharing data on progress is a necessary component of an overall accessibility program, but more important is how the data can be used to help the organization reach its overall accessibility objectives. To do this, the right people in the right places have to be able (and interested) to read the report information and ask the right questions about the results.

For example, if the reports show that progress is trending upward, but the curve is slow, leaders will want to understand what's occurring. Trending flat? Trending lower? They will question:

- Is there a particular product or set of products impacting progress, and why?
- Were other factors impacting performance? Acquired or purchased products included in the data? Vendor issues?
- How do we measure up in accessibility compared to competitors?

These questions should be answered by the stakeholder organizations being measured, not the messenger (reporters of the information), which is why it's good practice for the centralized accessibility function to share data with the lower levels of the stakeholder organizations. That's the way to get answers before the executives even ask the questions. Doing this allows the centralized accessibility function to prepare firm corrective action plans, which should include deadlines for resolving issues. Being proactive by providing the executives with information that explains the data and by setting deadlines for corrective action should establish a good relationship with them. This will prove valuable if resolutions take longer than the next reporting cycle or two.

8.1.8.1 **MOTIVATIONAL REPORTING**

Whenever several (or all) areas of an organization are measured with the same metric, the results can be reported in ways that articulate progress and performance relative to each other. Here's an example:

Organization Web Pages % Compliant

Fig. 8. Example of an IT accessibility report
by business area/department

If you were a senior executive of one of the stakeholder areas in the chart, how would you feel about your results compared with the other stakeholder areas? Well, if you are in Division 1, you would be a bit embarrassed that your area had the lowest compliance, right? To avoid being lowest in the future, you will probably drive your team pretty hard to improve your standing for the next reporting cycle.

Conversely, if you were the executive for distribution, you'd feel pretty good about the results. Egos at this level of an organization being what they are, you would also be thinking about how to ensure that your area maintains the highest percentage in the future.

In fact, if IT accessibility is a priority, reaching or maintaining certain results could be a performance measure tied to executive compensation.

8.2 TECHNICAL INFRASTRUCTURE FOR IT ACCESSIBILITY

Earlier I noted that this book is not a technical reference text for making products and services accessible. While that's true, I must spend some time on what I consider the technical resources (human and nonhuman) that an organization needs to fully and effectively integrate IT accessibility into its products, services, internal IT, and culture. In the interest of completeness, I will discuss this topic from the perspective of a large organization; however, what your organization needs depends on its size, nature, and other specific criteria.

8.2.1 CENTRALIZED ACCESSIBILITY TECHNICAL CONSULTING SERVICES FOR PRODUCT DEVELOPMENT

Look across the technical landscape of IT within a medium to large organization, and you will see an astounding diversity of technology used to bring products and services to the marketplace and to keep the organization's infrastructure running and on course. Given how broad and complex these two categories are, the central accessibility area must have people with deep technical skills (a.k.a., subject matter experts, or SMEs) to support this diversity of technologies. SMEs in this organization must be experts in both the technologies themselves and in enabling them for accessibility. They will be the "go-to" folks for the hard problems that cannot be solved by the developers or even the unit and subunit accessibility focal points throughout your organization.

To staff this expert team of internal consultants effectively, you will first have to understand and prioritize the IT technologies now in use (or planned) within your organization so that the team has the correct mix of skills. For example, if your organization is using a particular set of tools/technologies to develop large websites and many developers are involved in that activity, you need employees in the central accessibility area with deep programming and accessibility skills for those particular toolsets. These individuals should be able to provide consulting on difficult problems, as well be able to perform knowledge transfer to others in various forms. This builds organizational capacity across the developer communities within the organization. These individuals' duties would include the following:

- Providing consulting on difficult development problems
- Developing or procuring technology specific accessibility developer/tester training
- Developing or procuring other support materials, such as checklists, code examples, testing cases or techniques, and technical papers
- Keeping abreast of and evaluating web development tools, techniques, and the like, and sharing information about them throughout the community
- Keeping abreast of and communicating information about new or changing standards, regulations, and policies that could affect developers or the industry
- Consulting on related IT procurements
- Consulting on the architectural level
- Supporting sales and marketing (in the private sector)

When staffing these technical positions, you may not find people, internally or externally, with both expertise in the technical area and an understanding of accessibility within that technical area. However, it's easier to train someone with strong skills in a given technology about accessibility than vice versa. Of course, some time will be needed to build accessibility skills, but most senior-level technical professionals have plenty of experience in learning new technical areas, so acquiring expertise in accessibility shouldn't take long or be overly difficult.

8.2.2 **CENTRALIZED ACCESSIBILITY TECHNICAL CONSULTING SERVICES FOR TESTING PRODUCT**

While development and testing typically go hand in hand, the skills and tools needed for accessibility testing are different from those needed for development. Although there is certainly some overlap with development testing (developers typically must "unit test" their code before releasing it to product build streams, system testing, etc.), having an accessibility testing expert on the staff of the centralized accessibility organization is critical. The knowledge, skills, techniques, and tools for accessibility-testing are fairly extensive, so requiring an accessibility-development SME to be completely knowledgeable and current on test work, in addition to the extensive development aspects of IT accessibility, would be overtaxing. This could result in compromising the developers' ability to maintain the deep knowledge needed for both areas.

Accessibility testing, however, doesn't necessarily require technical skills specific to development technologies, because testing mainly deals with the user interface—what a user interacts with. Therefore, an accessibility-testing expert can theoretically work with multiple technologies. The testing expert doesn't need to delve too deeply into source code issues, but having some knowledge of coding can be helpful.

Here are the primary responsibilities of the accessibility-testing expert:

- Developing, obtaining, and maintaining accessibility-testing resources (tools, techniques, checklists, and other documentation)
- Accessibility-testing education and training
- Providing accessibility test-execution consulting
- Providing accessibility test plan and test cases consulting
- Evaluating accessibility test tools
- Executing accessibility tests

8.2.3 **ACCESSIBILITY TOOLS**

IT accessibility is a rapidly expanding field, with existing and emerging standards, regulations, and policies driving its growth to a significant degree. This means that there is more focus on IT accessibility, and therefore more of the public and private sectors are working to comply with accessibility. This growth also drives the development and availability of IT accessibility tools, which range from tools used by the individual developer or tester all the way up to enterprise-wide tools used to scan huge numbers of web pages. Some organizations may develop their own tools when no commercially available tools are available that support their technology needs.

IT accessibility tools have two main purposes:

- To facilitate the creation of accessible code, software products, web pages, and the like
- To validate the level of accessibility in end-user products and interfaces

The tools used are tailored to each of these purposes to a large degree, but there is overlap: the same tool can be used on the development side as well as the validation side. As a result, it is quite helpful if developers and testers work closely to coordinate tool selection. This helps ensure continuity of results and helps avoid compatibility issues caused by using different testing tools that yield slightly different test results.

8.2.3.1 **DEVELOPER/FACILITATION TOOLS**

Many types of IT accessibility tools can be used at various phases of the development process to assist the developer in producing code or content for meeting IT accessibility requirements. Most of these tools are designed with built-in rule sets or standards, such as WCAG 2.0, which help ensure that code meets the criteria set forth in the standards. Many tools provide the ability to select a standard rule set; some may offer the ability to modify or customize rules. Here are a few examples of developer tool types. Additional information is available on the web through the myriad of accessibility-related sites and blogs.

- Development environments with integrated accessibility authoring and checking tools. These are typically used in the development of websites or other software and can usually be scaled to accommodate many users.
- Content management systems (CMS) with accessibility-checking ability. CMS environments can include their own accessibility checkers or provide the ability to integrate third-party checking tools as part of the publication and release process.
- Inspection tools. These are developer tools that allow in-depth examination of either source or object code. Many of these are based on specific code technologies used for development.
- Manual inspection. Code review by peers or experts is not only useful but may be necessary if other development tools are not available.
- Accessibility design tools. These tools simulate for the developer how end users with particular disabilities (low vision, color blindness, etc.) will see a page or screen, so the developer can optimize the page code to address these user issues.
- Web page checkers. Desktop or web tools can check a page at a time for accessibility errors. Many are available and can address many technologies; many are free.
- Screen readers. This is a text-to-speech assistive-technology tool used by people who are blind or have low vision. Because screen readers are the actual tools used by the vision impaired, these tools are sometimes considered the final arbiter of accessibility. They can be used to check accessibility criteria that cannot be checked with other tools (e.g., JAWS, Voiceover, Window-Eyes).

8.2.3.2 **TEST TOOLS**

Although some accessibility testing is or should be done by the developer who codes or creates content, much of the accessibility testing typically occurs downstream, near or after the completion or release of the code. This is done by people independent of the developers who specialize in accessibility testing. The reason for accessibility testing is no different than that for other post-development testing: to ensure quality and independent confirmation of the developer's product. It's important to note that testers are confirming accessibility against the "object code," or what the end user interacts with, such as web pages and application screens, and not the source. Again, additional information is available on the web through myriad accessibility-related sites and blogs.

- Scan tools. In addition to manual accessibility testing, there are automated tools with built-in accessibility rule sets that "crawl" or "spider" entire websites looking for accessibility errors. Most can scan millions of pages and generate reports on the results down to the line number and error type. They also can generate higher-level summary reports, displaying information graphically. The information can then be sent to the owners of the website so the errors can be fixed by the page authors. Scan tools are not inexpensive, but they are powerful and can dramatically reduce common web-accessibility errors. Many tools now are capable of scanning documents such as PDFs on a website for accessibility.

  Please note that automated scanning is not a cure-all. While scan tools are continuing to improve in functionality, they are not technically capable of checking all accessibility criteria and can't scan for some elements that are meaningful to people with disabilities, like keyboard navigation, structure, and usability. Criteria such as these require human testers and will continue to require them for the foreseeable future.

- Web page checkers. Desktop or web tools can check a page at a time for accessibility errors upon code completion. Many are available and can address many technologies; many are free.
- Assistive technologies, or screen readers. People who are blind or have low vision use this text-to-speech assistive technology tool; screen readers can also be used to check for accessibility errors upon code completion. Because screen readers are the actual tools used by the vision impaired, these tools are sometimes considered the final arbiter of accessibility. They can be used to check accessibility criteria that cannot be checked with other tools.

8.3 ARCHITECTURE AND TECHNOLOGY PLATFORMS

Selecting and using accessibility-friendly technologies on which to build products, applications, or other IT is a key element in determining accessibility of products developed by your organization. Software architecture deals quite a bit with software "stacks." In simple terms, a software stack is a set of software subsystems, or components needed to deliver a fully functional solution, typically starting with an operating system on the lowest level, with the end-user product or service at the top, and various other components, or subsystems, in between. Assistive technologies, such as screen readers, interact with multiple layers of the stack, so understanding how the stack components interoperate with assistive technologies can be critical to IT accessibility and can determine the level of difficulty associated with the technical enablement of IT accessibility. With end users, different versions of any of the components in the stack can create interoperability problems, so care must be taken when choosing these components for development and test environments.

Consider, for example, an organization that serves federal agencies and decides to invest in and use a particular development tool suite for a new, large web project. The organization plans to use the suite for all future web projects, including migrating existing pages and applications to the new platform. The tool suite is robust in many ways: it simplifies web development and greatly reduces development time. However, accessibility criteria was not considered a priority in the selection process because the decision was made by software architects, and accessibility was not yet well ingrained in the culture of the organization's software architects. The suite has no accessibility development features or functions built into the tools, and it provides little to no documentation about how to code for accessibility. Because the technology is brand new, with its own set of custom development tools, the use of "of-the-shelf" accessibility development tools is not feasible, so accessibility coding must be done from scratch—assuming someone has already figured out how to code that technology to create an end result that is accessible. Also, whether the developer tools contained within the platform/tool suite are accessible to developers with disabilities can be an issue.

You can see how such an architectural decision can be devastating for an organization's IT strategy and bottom line. Such unfortunate scenarios can be avoided only if accessibility is considered by performing the following tasks:

- Including accessibility professionals throughout the selection process for defining the technical requirements and participating in technical evaluations (development and testing)
- Educating the organization's software architects on IT accessibility
- Ensuring that IT accessibility is a priority
- Ensuring that the procurement department understands IT accessibility and integrates appropriate terms and conditions into solicitations and contracts

One other aspect that can be helpful is to form a committee of your organization's software architects that can meet regularly to discuss accessibility-related topics relevant to the organization's IT strategies for products, services, or internal IT. This can help ensure that the left hand knows what the right hand is doing, which can help mitigate architectural issues or platform accessibility problems within the organization.

8.4 **PROCUREMENT**

Whether an organization is large or small, they have a high dependency of procured IT products and services and will to continue to have this dependency into the foreseeable future. These IT products and related services make up the majority of most organization's IT portfolios and are used in nearly every conceivable area or department. Nearly every year, the demand for IT continues to grow, which translates into lots of IT procurement activity and big IT spending.

While there has been progress across the IT industry in accessibility, unfortunately, a large number of available commercial off-the-shelf (COTS) products and services are still deficient in complying with accessibility technical standards. As discussed earlier in the book, there are lots of reasons for these deficiencies.

Beyond the procurement of COTS offerings comes development services procurement—that is, companies that develop custom IT solutions such as websites, web or software applications, or other IT either from scratch or built from an existing "base" platform. The lack of progress in this area is particularly troubling and carries with it significant risk, both for the vendor side as well as to the procuring organization. This is especially true for government sector or other places where accessibility is a well-known requirement, and one that has potentially negative consequences if not implemented, but unfortunately one not well managed or enforced in the procurement life cycle. Again, lots of reasons why this continues to occur, but with the right knowledge, methods, management, and tools, one can obtain highly accessible results.

8.4.1 **IT INTEGRATING IT ACCESSIBILITY INTO THE PROCUREMENT LIFE CYCLE**

Procurement is a specialized field, and IT procurement represents yet another level of specialization. When IT accessibility is folded in as well, another layer of complexity/effort is introduced and needs to be addressed in a logical, methodical fashion , meaning *integrating IT accessibility into the IT procurement life cycle.*

In chapter 7, I identified some key areas of procurement in which IT accessibility plays a role. And earlier, in chapter 8, I discussed the importance of integrating IT accessibility into processes where IT accessibility plays a role. So we will now take a deeper dive into IT procurement processes, to look at the points of integration for IT accessibility and some examples of specific tasks that should be undertaken at the integration points.

8.4.2 **THE IT PROCUREMENT LIFE CYCLE**

I don't want to endorse any single IT procurement life cycle that includes IT accessibility, as many examples of them can be found with a web search. Also, your organization may already have one or several that it uses (but perhaps without IT accessibility activates fully integrated).

Figure 9 shows a high-level schematic of a simplified IT procurement life cycle that addresses the basics and which can be used for both COTS or a vendor development project. As you can see, most of the life cycle phases apply to both types of IT procurements, but you will note that there are branches when development services specific phases deviate from COTS due to differences in actions/tasks.

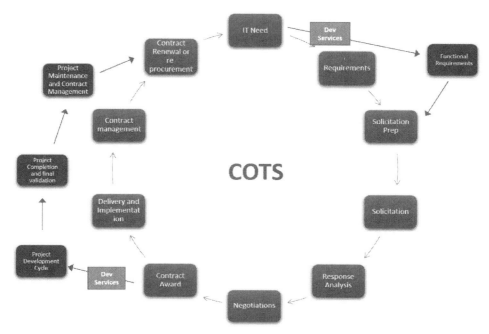

Fig. 9. Example of a IT procurment life cycle COTS or dev

8.4.2.1 UNDERSTANDING THE NEED FOR IT ACCESSIBILITY IN PROCURED PRODUCTS/SERVICES

The first thing that needs to be done in an IT procurement with regard to accessibility is to determine the applicability of accessibility requirements to the product or service being procured. An IT-procurement organization may want to establish some guideline criteria as an aid in determining when IT accessibility criteria apply to the procurement. The table that follows is an example of a procurement guideline for applying IT accessibility criteria.

Table 8.1 IT Accessibility Procurement Types

IT procurement type	Examples	Is IT accessibility procurement criteria needed?
Direct use of IT	The procurement of • Software used on public websites • Software used by employees in the performance of their work • Copy machines that will be used by employees • Services to develop websites used by employees or the public • Externally hosted websites or services used by the public or employees	Yes
Direct but insignificant use of IT	The procurement of specific software with no administrative or public user interface	Maybe
Indirect use of IT	The procurement of • Services delivered through a website or telephone system • Services that may be delivered through social media such as Facebook pages or through web-based multimedia or videos • Training or technical support that may be delivered through electronic handbooks, forms, or a web-based or telephone information system • Transaction services that may require the public to interact with IT through interoperable controls, video screens, menus, or websites, as in the use of a debit card reader or ticket kiosk	Maybe
No IT use	Purchase of office supplies	No

Also, I use a rule of thumb that I found useful: if the product/service has a IT user interfaces used by the procuring organization (including administrative interfaces) in some capacity or by members of the public, and those interfaces are the primary means of using the product or service, then IT accessibility would apply.

If during a procurement, a vendor claims that the IT user interface does not fall under this rule of thumb, or listed above, have them provide justification as to why they are making this claim, and examine this information carefully in the vendor response analysis.

8.4.3 **IT ACCESSIBILITY REQUIREMENTS/FUNCTIONAL REQUIREMENTS**

Typically, an IT procurement life cycle begins with a need to solve a kind of problem by some part of the organization. From there, requirements are based on the particular need. At this early stage, it is crucial that IT accessibility criteria are imbedded in the requirements document, as their exclusion will potentially preclude IT accessibility in the other phases, likely resulting in an inaccessible deliverable.

At this phase, the most important thing is to include, by reference or directly, the appropriate criteria, such as accessibility technical standards (e.g., WCAG 2.0) and or any other accessibility criteria that the solution must meet. In most cases, citing the standards, regulations, and policies is sufficient as long as suppliers can also access the details. If your organization has developed an internal standard for use, access to the technical specifications for that standard will also need to be provided.

Note the requirements or functional requirements documents relate to the *actual functioning of the product* and not the tasks a vendor needs to fulfill. Nonfunctional vendor requirements are suited for the subsequent phases of the procurement—or if the organization is doing a statement of work (SOW) IT procurement, which lumps functional and vendor performance into a single, often less formal document. If doing an SOW, you would likely also want to include *vendor requirements* in that document so the vendor fully understands what is expected (I will discuss this shortly).

8.4.4 **DEVELOPING THE IT ACCESSIBILITY SOLICITATION LANGUAGE AND DOCUMENTS**

The IT procurement solicitation is one of the most important elements of the procurement life cycle. It should not only tell vendors what is required from the deliverable that procurement is seeking but provide valuable insight and information as to a vendor's capabilities: ability to deliver, references, pricing, information about their company, and, if done correctly, a broad perspective on IT accessibly and their present and future positions on IT accessibility.

Of course, it's a no-brainer that the language should include requirements such as accessibility technical standards (e.g., WCAG) or other accessibility criteria, but is the IT accessibility language and requested information be structured in a way that answers these basic questions:

1. COTS. How accessible are a vendor's offerings?
2. Development services. How well can a vendor develop accessible solutions (websites/web apps, app customization, etc.)
3. How can I know if a vendor has the knowledge, processes, and commitment to produce accessible products and services, now and in the future?

Standard language can be developed that can be included in all solicitations where meeting IT accessibility criteria is required. If crafted properly, this language can be used in all solicitations.

Below is an example of standard IT procurement accessibility language that is currently being used by the Texas Department of Information Resources (DIR):

Electronic and Information Resources (EIR) Accessibility

Products, applications, and websites that will be used by Texas state employees or members of the public must comply with EIR accessibility technical standards as defined in 1 TAC 206, 1 TAC 213, and Web Content Accessibility Guidelines (WCAG) 2.0 level AA. Accurate product Voluntary Product Accessibility Templates (VPATs) are required for Commercial Off-the-Shelf (COTS) offerings included in this contract. If development services are included, vendors will be required to complete the Vendor Accessibility Services Development Information Request (VASDIR) or other documents as requested that describe vendor's ability to produce accessible offerings. The Successful Respondent shall provide a solution that is compliant with the above referenced standards, and provide satisfactory responses on the VASDIR or other documents. Respondent shall complete:

> Attachment C: ICT Accessibility Policy Assessment;
> Attachment D: VPAT; and
> Attachment E: Vendor Accessibility Development Services Information Request.

Per **Table 4:** Response Package 1 Files, the Respondent shall include completed above-referenced attachments in Response Package 1.

Note: As an alternative to completing Attachment: D: VPAT, Respondents may provide external links to VPAT information. DIR requests Respondents provide electronic downloads of the relevant information from the external link, and that the electronic information be included in their Response Package 1. Hardcopies of VPATs is not required.

Note that Texas also references its administrative rules in addition to WCAG as there are provisions within those rules that vendors need to pay attention to (although many don't—to their detriment).

Also note the use of the word "accurate" in the instructions for VPAT completion. This and "credible evidence" are important terms when analyzing VPATs and will be discussed in the response analysis phase section.

With regard to non-COTS, DIR requests, "credible evidence of the Vendor's capability or ability to produce accessible electronic and information resources" really comes into play. If there was something like a VPAT that covered this class of IT procurements, that would be ideal , but there isn't, so DIR created their own, called the Vendor Accessibility Development Services Information Request (VADSIR), used to collect preliminary "credible evidence."

Vendor Accessibility Development Services Information Request

1. Vendor Information

Vendor Name: ▨	Submitter Name : ▨		Date: ▨
Email: ▨	Phone: (▨) ▨		
Address: ▨	City: ▨	State: ▨	ZIP: ▨

2. Instructions

Complete this form if your company or organization is responding to a Texas Agency solicitation that includes one or more of the following Information and Communications Technologies (ICT) offering types:

Website development services

Web Application Development Services

Custom development services as part of an integrated solution.

Client based software application development services

Other software development services containing one or more user interfaces (end user, admin, etc.)

Please direct any questions regarding this request to the DIR Procurement Office.

3. Please respond to the questions below as applicable

1. Describe or provide documentation regarding your organization's key business processes that include the integration of ICT accessibility activities. (Examples are product development, procurement, HR, etc.): ▨

2. Describe the skills and training resources that your organization uses (internal or third party) to develop and produce accessible ICT offerings: ▨

3. Describe the development and test tools used within your organization to produce accessible ICT offerings. Provide examples of typical project test cases for accessibility and examples of how test results are documented: ▨

4. Describe your organizations corrective actions process(es) or system(s) for documenting, tracking, and resolving accessibility issues/defects: ▨

5. Describe alternate methods for ICT products that are not compliant with accessibility technical standards. (example: 24hour/7day/week toll free phone support number): ▨

6. Provide links to example websites or other examples of ICT work that your organization has produced that meet accessibility technical standards such as US Section 508, or WCAG 2.0 AA: ▨

The vendor responses to the VADSIR form are extremely valuable and open the door to additional followup questions should procurement choose to enter into negotiations with the vendor. I will cover this as well in the response analysis phase section.

Now let's consider the last of the three questions: How can I know if a vendor has the knowledge, processes, and commitment to produce accessible products and services now and in the future?

While PDAA was covered in chapter 4, it was originally derived to be used a procurement tool that allows procurement organizations to understand how well accessibility is woven into vendor organizations' processes and culture. It is based on an organization having a solid accessibility policy on the accessibility of the products/services it sells. The idea behind organization-wide policy is simple: if an organization has a good IT accessibility policy, and if the organization follows that policy, then the accessibility levels of the products/services it offers will improve over time.

So, to review ...

The PDAA Maturity Model is based on six simple core criteria, each related to a key governance element of an organization:

	Core criteria
Policy creation	1. Develop, implement, and maintain an ICT accessibility policy.
Organization	2. Establish and maintain an organizational structure that enables and facilitates progress in ICT accessibility.
Business process	3. Integrate ICT accessibility criteria into key phases of development, procurement, acquisitions, and other relevant business processes.

	Core criteria
Compliance planning	4. Provide processes for addressing inaccessible ICT.
Training	5. Ensure the availability of relevant ICT accessibility skills within (or to) the organization.
Communication	6. Make information regarding ICT accessibility policy, plans, and progress available to customers.

Maturity levels are measured on a linear scale with three states of maturity:

- Launch state
- Integrate state
- Optimize state

The descriptions of how these states apply to the six-core-criteria model are defined within the PDAA maturity matrix, below:

	Core criteria	Launch	Integrate	Optimize
1.	Develop, implement, and maintain an ICT accessibility policy.	Have an ICT accessibility policy.	Have appropriate plans in place to implement and maintain the policy.	Establish metrics and track progress towards achieving compliance to the policy.
2.	Establish and maintain an organizational structure that enables and facilitates progress in ICT accessibility.	Develop an organization-wide governance system.	Designate one or more individuals responsible for implementation.	Implement reporting/ decision mechanism and maintain records.

Core criteria	Launch	Integrate	Optimize
3. Integrate ICT accessibility criteria into key phases of development, procurement, acquisitions, and other relevant business processes.	Identify candidate processes for criteria integration.	Implement process changes.	Integrate fully into all key processes.
4. Provide processes for addressing inaccessible ICT.	Create plans that include dates for compliance of inaccessible ICT.	Provide alternative means of access until the ICT is accessible; implement corrective actions process for handling accessibility technical issues and defects	Maintain records of identified inaccessible ICT, corrective action, and tracking.
5. Ensure the availability of relevant ICT accessibility skills within (or to) the organization.	Define skills/job descriptions.	Identify existing resources that match up and address gaps.	Manage progress in acquiring skills and allocating qualified resources.
6. Make information regarding ICT accessibility policy, plans, and progress available to customers.	Make Launch level information available.	Make "integrate"-level information available.	Make "optimize"-level information available.

To obtain the level of vendor PDAA maturity, a form is included in the solicitation documentation. Today, it is in the form of an Excel spreadsheet that vendors are required to complete. As a vendor completes the form, the scores for each response are tallied at the bottom of the spreadsheet, generating a bar graph result that depicts the overall stage of maturity in which a vendor lies. An example of some of the questions and the bar graph is below:

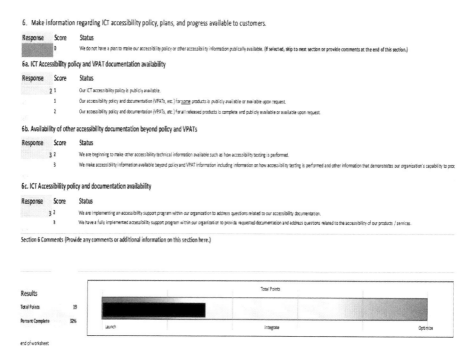

Fig. 10. Bottom section of PDAA form showing last question and maturity-level results bar

There are multiple ways that this information can be used in the response analysis and negotiating phases; this will be discussed shortly.

There are other IT accessibility maturity models available in both the public and private sector, some freely available and others at a fee. Because many of these contain more detailed questions, I believe that they are better suited for internal audit purposes rather than as a procurement tool; however, some of the questions contained within them can be used to obtain additional information from the PDAA results, if desired. For more information on PDAA, read the two-part series on the NASCIO website, at www.nascio.org/pdaa.

8.4.4.1 IT ACCESSIBILITY SOLICITATION DOCUMENTS SUMMARY

Armed with responses to any combination of these three information-request types, and assuming there is someone within the procuring organization that understands how to analyze the results, the procuring organization will be well positioned to make intelligent decisions about the accessibility of the products/services being procured and the organization that plans to deliver them.

8.4.5 ANALYZING THE ACCESSIBILITY RESPONSE DOCUMENTS

Once you have received the responses, the next step is to analyze how the vendors have responded to your IT accessibility solicitation language and documents.

It's important to keep in mind that the documents as submitted are in essence "self-reported" information. Some vendors have a very high degree of IT accessibility knowledge and documentation, and others not so much. In vendor's anxiousness to win the bid and a contract, I see many "overly optimistic" responses that, upon further examination, can not be substantiated by supporting documentation and accuracy can vary wildly from vendor to vendor, or document to document. In this section, I will provide some guidance as to what to look for, what are some of the "red flags," and what follow-up information might be needed to solidify the quality of the IT accessibility response.

8.4.5.1 ANALYZING VPATS

VPATs were originally developed to address accessibility compliance reporting to the original US Section 508, which went into effect in 2000. And, at the time of my writing of this second edition of my book, procurement organizations and vendors are still experiencing problems in both the development and analysis of these documents. VPAT 2.0 is now being used, which will be improved in that it addresses WCAG success criteria. However, there is little information required which documents how the information in the completed VPAT was substantiated, validated, certified, and so on. And why they continued to use the term "voluntary" still eludes me. What is it that makes the document voluntary exactly? If it is a required document in the procurement process, it is required, isn't it? (I have digressed a little. Sorry.)

The issue with VPATs is that there are no prescribed process/procedures for how to complete them and who should complete them. I've seen VPATs completed by developers, sales teams, marketing teams, attorneys, and even resellers completing them for the manufacturers it represents rather than requesting the VPATs from the manufacturers!

I will say that many of the larger IT companies who do business in the government sector tend to do a pretty good job on their VPAT documentation, and for the most part, the information can be trusted, as these companies typically have accessibility testing programs and understand the ramifications of supplying inaccurate documents in government or even private-sector bids.

But still, there are many vendors of all sizes that do not, and if you know what to look for in VPAT, this is readily apparent. Here are a few examples of red flags to look for:

- Vendor asks, "What is a VPAT?"
- No VPATs are provided when IT accessibility is applicable.
- No VPATs are provided, but global, nonspecific accessibility statements are included.
- There are incomplete/missing sections or the use of "N/A" (not applicable) in areas of the VPAT criteria that are known to be applicable. (Frequently missing example: 1194.41 Information, Documentation and Support.)
- VPATs are created by a reseller and not the product's manufacturer.

- "Supports" or "N/A" is listed for all responses in the "Supporting Features" column.
- No information in the "Remarks" column are provided that describe response in the "Supporting Features" column.
- Product name, contact, evaluation methods, and other information are missing from the VPAT form.

If any of these red flags pop up, its time to probe the vendor deeper. Here are a few questions you might ask:

- What tools/methods were used to test and complete the VPAT?
- What client platforms (operating systems (including mobile), browsers, assistive technologies, and versions of all of those) were used as test environments?
- Can the vendor provide a copy of the accessibility test plan for the product?
- Can the vendor provide the results of the accessibility testing?
- What issues were found, and are there corrective actions in place to resolve them in this or a subsequent release (and when)?

If the vendor cannot answer these questions satisfactorily (as determined by a person knowledgeable in IT accessibility), assume the product is not accessible, and factor that into your overall procurement assessment. There is no need for you as the customer to perform any accessibility testing on the product, as you will waste a lot of time and money to learn what you already know.

8.4.5.2 ANALYZING THE VENDOR ACCESSIBILITY DEVELOPMENT SERVICES INFORMATION REQUEST (VADSIR)

As mentioned earlier, VPATs are associated with COTS offerings, so when soliciting vendors to develop custom IT, such as a website or an application, there is no standard reporting tool that reports on vendors' abilities and capabilities to create accessible IT. This is why at the Texas Department of Information Resources, we created the VADSIR to do just that. The information requested is more qualitative in nature; therefore, it is important that someone pretty familiar with IT accessibility in development reviews and evaluates the vendor's responses.

Some problem areas that should raise concern in a vendor's accessibility capabilities:

- Lack of accessibility specific information on how accessibility is integrated into their development life cycle process(es)
- Lack of accessibility specific information on IT accessibility training and resources, (such WCAG, US Section 508 accessibility testing, etc.)
- Lack of accessibility specific information on development and testing tools used to create customer IT (WAVE, JAWS, accessibility code validators, authoring tools, test environments, etc.)
- Lack of information on accessibility defect identification/tracking, remediation during the development process
- Inability to provide examples of prior work where accessibility was a requirement, or prior work examples provided contain significant accessibility issues
- Vendor home page has significant accessibility issues

Again, if the vendor responses to the VADSIR are not satisfactory, selecting such a vendor should be seen as a significant risk to the procuring organization for the reasons mentioned in previous chapters.

8.4.5.3 ANALYZING THE PDAA VENDOR SELF-ASSESSMENT

The third accessibility component for evaluation is the response to the PDAA form. The PDAA is scored from 0 to 100 points, along the maturity matrix continuum, and serves several purposes in the overall evaluation of a vendor.

The primary purpose for use by procurement organizations is to help assess a vendor's ability to produce accessible offerings. Logically, if a vendor scores high on the maturity matrix, then one should be able to assume a high degree of confidence in vendor's VPAT, VADSIR, and other accessibility documentation (barring any red flags in those documents). Conversely, if a vendor scores low on the matrix, the maturity of its program is still not where it should be, and the other document responses should be more closely scrutinized. An IT-procurement organization should pay particular attention to a vendor response with a high PDAA score when there appear to be significant issues with the other response documents. This could mean that the vendor is "overly optimistic" (which I say politely) in their accessibility maturity. All this analysis can be factored into the selection process and warrant requests to the vendor for information that supports their responses.

Another use for the PDAA response is to track vendor progress, should a vendor respond to multiple solicitations over time. If used this way, IT procurement should hopefully be seeing improvement in the PDAA scores as vendor implements its accessibility program. A lack of improvement over time might indicate that the vendor is not that interested in IT accessibility. At some point, if this is also reflected in the products and services it provides, this lack of improvement might result in a procuring organization choosing not to do business with that vendor.

In addition to use by IT procurement organizations in solicitations, IT vendors who have scored low on the matrix can use the PDAA core criteria and results to build and guide the implement its own organization-wide accessibility program/initiatives to help them achieve more accessible offerings over the long term.

8.4.6 APPLYING SCORING METHODOLOGIES TO IT ACCESSIBILITY RESPONSES

Now that all of this IT accessibility documentation/information has been acquired, how can an IT procurement organization factor it into the solicitation responses?

In many cases, a scoring methodology has been applied to the solicitation. The scoring criteria are typically established in the planning phase and communicated to the vendors at the beginning of the bid process. For example, a scoring methodology for evaluating vendor responses based on the solicitation criteria might look like this:

Price	40%
References	15%
Vendor performance	20%
HUB	10%
IT accessibility	15%
Total	100%

These values must be negotiated and established before the solicitations going out for bid. In this example IT accessibility will be scored for up to 15 percent of each vendor bid. This, like the other percentages, should be flexible, depending on the products or services being solicited. For example, the breakdown above might be for accounting system software, highly specialized and for use by limited users; however, for a solicitation for a website development service vendor for a public, high-volume website, the breakdown may want to have more emphasis on IT accessibility, given the nature of the procurement, and look more like this:

Price	30%
References	15%
Vendor performance	20%

HUB	10%
IT accessibility	25%
Total	100%

In addition to the percentage of IT accessibility in the total score, how are each of these three elements (or two depending on the product/services solicited) scored, and how do those scores roll up to the total accessibility score?

Here are scoring systems that I typically use in a preliminary assessment of a vendor solicitation response.

VPAT documentation	Rating of 0–3
100 pts	3- Credible, accessibility documentation for all or most products included in the bid response. Response shows strong understanding of accessibility by vendor.
60 pts	2- Questionable, incomplete or inaccurate accessibility documentation most likely not supported by testing.
15 pts	1- Accessibility documentation indicates very limited to no knowledge of accessibility.
0 pts	0- Accessibility documentation required but not provided.

VADSIR responses	
0	UNSAT—No completed VADSIR submitted but is applicable OR responses indicate insufficient knowledge of web accessibility to produce accessible websites/web applications.
50	Low SAT—Responses indicate a deficiency of knowledge in key areas of website accessibility that significantly impacts the vendor's ability to develop and deliver accessible websites/applications.
100	SAT—Responses indicate an acceptable level of knowledge, skills, and processes to produce accessible websites/web applications.

PDAA scoring	
0–100	As calculated on the PDAA assessment form.

Taking all three of these elements (VPATs, VADSIR, PDAA) into account, a final score can be derived by averaging the results of the percentages across the two or three elements. The example below uses all three elements (VPATs, VADSIR, PDAA), and each of the three elements is weighted equally (i.e., 1/3), for the sake of simplicity.

Vendor	Dev Services Rating	VPAT Rating	PDAA Score (0-100)	Accessibility Score (Up to 100%)	Overall Satisfactory Rating	Comments
Vendor name	Satisfactory	2	61	73.67%	High	Description of accessibility plans and integration into its Technical Solution appear comprehensive and well documented. VPAT submission: For the single VPAT provided, vendor should provide additional details on the exceptions listed. There also appear to be other COTS products included in the vendor response which may require VPATs and for which VPATs were not present. These include, but not limited to: XXX or its components thereof or any COTS or customized COTS products / services with user interfaces intended for Texas state employees or members of the public. Vendor should provide.

Fig. 11. Vendor procurement scoring results

The final accessibility score is 73.5; using the example overall result scoring metric (below), the submission is rated as high.

Scoring results	Overall satisfactory rating
0–35%	Low
36–70%	Medium
71–100%	High

From here, it is a simple calculation to integrate the total accessibility score into the final overall solicitation score, using the example with accessibility being valued at 15 percent of the total solicitation:

$$73.5\% \text{ (accessibility score)} \times 0.15 \text{ (value in solicitation)}$$
$$= 0.11 \text{ or } 11\% \text{ or } 11 \text{ points out of the possible } 15$$
$$\text{points allocated for IT accessibility.}$$

So now, not only has a value for the levels of accessibility a vendor has been established, but the results serve as topics for discussion and further information needs in the negotiation phase, should the vendor be selected to move forward to that phase. This is where more specific questions related to the responses/ratings should be asked and answered.

8.4.7 **FOLLOW-UP QUESTIONS TO THE IT ACCESSIBILITY RESPONSES IN CONTRACT NEGOTIATIONS**

Given that all of the IT accessibility information collected so far is vendor self-reported, the negotiations phase is where the procurement organization can and should ask more detailed "follow up" questions to validate vendor solicitation responses. The goal here is to obtain as much information as needed to truly understand if VPATs are accurate, or that the vendor can produce accessible IT and that it has appropriate governance models in place to help ensure that IT accessibility is baked into the processes and culture of the organization—and without the IT procurement organization (customer) having to perform extensive testing to validate the response for themselves.

Let me be clear about this: the burden of proof for substantiating vendor accessibility documentation resides with the vendor, not the customer! And by asking the right follow-up questions, possessing the knowledge to interpret the responses and appropriate contract language, customer-based testing can be significantly reduced for any phase of the procurement.

8.4.7.1 **VPAT SUBMISSION FOLLOW-UP**

As I mentioned earlier, there can be a lot of variability in the accuracy of VPATs. You can best understand how accurate vendor VPAT is by requesting additional information about how the responses were derived. For example:

- Was the VPAT completed using the results of accessibility testing by someone knowledgeable in accessibility testing?

  If the answer is "no," assume the product is not accessible, and use that information in the purchasing.

- If "yes" to the above question, then what kind of accessibility testing was performed/what tools and test environment were used?

- o If the response doesn't include things like "screen readers" (or even a specific screen reader like "JAWS"), accessibility page checkers (e.g., WAVE, or other known accessibility-validation tools) this indicates the product was not accessibility tested, and the VPAT is likely inaccurate.

- If "yes" to testing, can the vendor provide the test results, test plans/cases?

  - o There may be business reasons why a vendor may choose not to provide this kind of internal information. You, as a customer, could offer to sign a nondisclosure agreement to obtain this information, but the vendor may or may not be willing or able to do that.
  - o What issues were found, and are there corrective actions in place to resolve them in this or a subsequent release—and when?

- If the vendor still cannot supply this information, you should request a letter of certification from them stating something to the effect of "the product was tested in accordance with generally accepted accessibility testing practices (including visual inspection and with an assistive technology) and that the information in the VPAT(s) is accurate."

Note: The letter should support the level of compliance as documented in the VPAT(s) and should not be written as a statement of "full compliance", unless the product is in full compliance, of course.

If the vendor is unwilling to provide such a letter, and the VPAT looked sketchy to begin with, then again assume the product is not very accessible and base your business decisions on that. Certainly, don't waste your time and money testing the damn thing!

In all fairness, I do not advocate total elimination of customer (or customer-paid third-party) testing. Depending on the asset being procured, the customer can and probably should "sniff" test in places to validate the accuracy of the vendor test documentation or their letter of certification and to ensure there are no assistive technology interoperability issues within the customer's solution platforms.

8.4.7.2 **VADSIR SUBMISSION FOLLOW-UP**

The completed VADSIR form allows vendors to respond in a more open-ended way so analysis of the results will be more qualitative rather than quantitative. Therefore, it's important that whoever does the analysis has a more strategic perspective of IT accessibility both organizational and technical.

Earlier, we looked at some of problematic responses to the VADSIR; knowing those should serve as a guide as to what additional information is needed to validate or challenge the responses. The ultimate goal here is to have the highest degree of confidence that a vendor can and will produce an accessible IT deliverable.

So, if in responding to the VADSIR, a vendor cannot provide supporting information to its original responses during this phase of the procurement related to the following:

- Accessibility integration into key processes, such as its development processes
- Response to skills/training with little to no mention of accessibility relating topics that an accessibility SME would recognize
- Tools used in development/testing of their work products have little to no relevance to IT accessibility
- Inability to explain why a site developed and listed for you to inspect has accessibility issues or the vendor's own website has accessibility issues

If any of these conditions are present, it is less than advisable to consider this vendor to develop accessible IT. That said, always inquire if someone knowledgeable about the vendor's accessibility programs has responded to the form. A sales rep may have completed it, having little to no knowledge of IT accessibility or a vendor's IT accessibility initiatives.

8.4.7.3 PDAA SUBMISSION FOLLOW-UP

In many ways, follow-up questions to the PDAA responses are similar to how the VADSIR is handled, but they are different in that you are trying to ascertain how imbedded IT accessibility is in the vendor organization's culture. See if you are apprehensive about a vendor's maturity levels based on responses to these requests:

- IT accessibility policy. Ask them to share it and analyze it for both content and authenticity.
- IT accessibility organizational structure. Ask them to provide organizational charts to see where the main accessibility function resides and if the areas which you as a customer does business with also contain accessibility staff.
- The integration of accessibility into its key business process, most importantly, its product development life cycle. Ask them to provide documentation of their processes, showing how and where accessibility fits in the relevant phases.
- Its processes for addressing inaccessible IT of its products/ services. Ask them how accessibility issues are classified and addressed in their corrective actions subprocesses of development, as well as any alternative means of access that they might have.
- IT accessibility training and skills currency addressed at an organizational level. Ask them to provide documentation on related technical training programs for development and test organizations, as well as information or any general awareness training for all employees; ask if accessibility is formally included in employee performance plans as relevant.

How a vendor responds to the above questions will indicate how open and willing they are to share information about their organization's accessibility initiatives. Again, it's important to realize that some of the information requests might be considered confidential or "internal use only," so obtaining them might require a CDA or NDA. If the vendor is totally unwilling to provide any of the information based on your additional questions, and the original responses again seem "overly optimistic" based on other IT accessibility response data points used in the evaluation (VPAT quality or VADSIR responses), caution is advised.

8.4.8 IT ACCESSIBILITY CRITERIA IN FINAL CONTRACT/SOW LANGUAGE

Assuming that a vendor has been selected that performed well in responding to the IT accessibility criteria in the original solicitation and was able to effectively answer your follow-up questions in the negotiations process, the next step will be to ensure that the necessary language around IT accessibility for the product/service being procured is included in the final contract, SOW, and other documentation. The language should be such that there is very little ambiguity so that the vendor understands precisely what is expected and when.

Because of the differences between an IT procurement for a COTS product/service and a non-COTS service, such as an IT development service, the language for each will have differences as well.

Here are some things to consider when crafting contract/SOW language around IT accessibility:

- Is the accessibility technical standard that you want the deliverable to meet defined?
- Are there formal checkpoints throughout the development cycle to monitor accessibility progress (non-COTS)?

- Have you included review/approval authority for accessibility test plans, tools, and platforms used for testing (non-COTS)?
- How and when will accessibility test results documentation be provided (non-COTS)?
- Is there a corrective actions process defined?
- Is there specific language related to accessibility remedies and warranties?
- Is there language that allows requests for additional information as needed that supports the vendor solicitation response documents?
- Is there a provision to provide a pre-deliverable delivery letter stating that accessibility development and testing was performed in accordance with generally accepted accessibility practices (including visual inspection and with an assistive technology), that the test results and other documentation supplied to your organization are accurate, and that the deliverable complies with the specified accessibility standards (or cites exceptions where it doesn't with a corrective actions plan)?

If the contract/SOW includes language that addresses these questions, the vendor understands and concurs with this language, and you were satisfied with the solicitation response documentation and follow up, there should be a high level of confidence that the vendor will provide or produce a highly accessible deliverable.

8.4.9 **IT ACCESSIBILITY TESTING OF PROCURED OFFERINGS**

In the original edition of this book was published, I strongly supported the idea of extensive and thorough IT accessibility testing of vendor procured products and services to validate that these deliverables met the accessibility standards as defined in project requirements. But since that time, my thinking evolved in that regard.

I'm a car guy, and I love car analogies, no doubt a carryover from my days in the world of industrial design, where car analogies were often used to convince engineers or management why a product should be designed a certain way. Therefore, let me use one to make an important point about accessibility testing.

Let's say that you are in the market for a new car. One of the important features that you would be interested in is safety, obviously.

You do your research—price, brand, performance, style, warranty, and then, of course, safety. The car you select has the right blend of all these things. You look at the safety ratings/certifications, like what you read, so you buy it.

Now that you have acquired the vehicle, would you be expected to ensure the safety specs on the car are true and accurate? Airbag deployments, side-impact reinforcement, crumple zones, etc.? How would you go about doing this, drive your car into a tree at 60 mph?

Of course not. In fact, the manufacturer has already performed extensive testing of the vehicle's safety systems and has certified that the vehicle meets these standards, and to what degree.

So, given the analogy above, is it reasonable for your vendors to expect the customer to spend its money and resources to perform comprehensive accessibility testing on their products and online services?

I would argue no, it's not. Again, I say that the *burden of proof belongs to the vendor, not the customer.* Here are some technical reasons why:

1. Testing needs to be performed throughout a development process, starting at unit test, to identify and correct issues early. Customer testing would typically be performed far downstream in the development or post-development process making such testing a very late way to identify issues and have them resolved. This is especially true for large, complex applications, so the likelihood that fixes would be integrated into the version a customer buys is low. ("We'll put it in the next release.") If such testing efforts have not been

performed during the development of the COTS product or development deliverable, it is likely not to be very accessible, so why would the customer spend its resources to learn the obvious?

2. IT accessibility testing typically requires a deep understanding of the product/service to be tested to develop test plans and execute those plans. This means knowledge transfer from the vendor to the customer and assumes a willingness by the vendor to do so.

3. Testing may require a specialized IT environment to install and test the IT asset that the customer has yet to deploy. In some cases, access to a vendor site where an instance of product/service is installed may be provided and hopefully complies with security polices of the customer organization.

4. And last but not least, there are the cost considerations (human resources + time + test tools + documentation) associated with proper testing, either through a customer internal accessibility testing facilities or the use of a third party.

When these aspects are considered, it is obvious where responsibility for pre-delivery testing should reside. And the contract/SOW needs to reflect this.

Let me also say that I do not advocate total elimination of customer testing (or customer-paid third-party testing), but if the vendor's test results are deemed comprehensive and accurate by a knowledgeable IT accessibility professional and all of the vendor's solicitation-response documentation and customer follow-up questions (which I've described) have been adequately addressed, it may be that customer "sniff" testing in the customer environment is all that is needed. The correct contract language is described above.

8.4.10 **DOCUMENTING IT ACCESSIBILITY EXCEPTIONS**

Sadly, at the time of this writing, there still exists a large gap in the IT marketplace for fully accessible COTS products and services. Therefore, there will be times where the procurement of a particular product that solves a particular problem is not accessible (or not fully accessible). However, the need for the product outweighs the risks of the product not being accessible. In such cases, the procuring organization should have an IT accessibility exception process, which includes documentation for why procuring an inaccessible piece of IT was required and other information, such as plans/dates/releases for full compliance other aspects, as required by the organization. One key element of the exception is the approval signature of a responsible executive in the organization who understands why the exception was made and accepts the risk of the product being not accessible.

To be most effective, the time to file the exception is before a contract is signed. That way, the executive responsible for signing (and accepting the risk of) the exception can do the following:

- Request additional information about the exception
- Modify the contract
- Reject the exception, preventing the contract from being signed, which could result in rebidding the procurement, reconsideration of suppliers in the original bid, or even cancellation of the procurement

8.5 **ACQUISITIONS**

As scenario 5 at the end of chapter 5 shows, acquiring another company can have a significant impact on your organization's IT accessibility levels and progress, creating new risks and ultimately affecting the bottom line. Therefore accessibility criteria must be included in assessment work alongside more traditional items, such as financials, product portfolio, and staffing. Factoring in the findings of an IT accessibility assessment has several important advantages.

8.5.1 BASIC IT ACCESSIBILITY QUESTIONS DURING ACQUISITIONS

Asking a few basic questions of a potential acquisition is an excellent way to gauge the status of its accessibility programs and compliance levels.

- Can the company demonstrate that it has an IT accessibility program for product development? Does it have internal IT?
- Does the company create VPATs for its product offerings? Are they accurate?
- Can the company demonstrate how it measures and tracks accessibility progress? What are the results?
- What is the level of the company's accessibility maturity (the PDAA questionnaire results?)

Assuming that IT accessibility is important to your organization, the responses to these questions should be extremely helpful in weighing the acquisition and paving the way for a deeper look, if necessary.

8.5.2 NEGOTIATING THE ACQUISITION PRICE

Let's say, for example, that a main reason for an acquisition is to integrate the candidate company's products and proprietary technologies into your organization's products (as bundles of components or other forms of software integration) and product portfolio. Your organization does an accessibility assessment of the candidate's components and products and determines that they are not very accessible. It will require a significant amount of effort, time, and expense to bring these components and products to a usable level of accessibility before they can be integrated or sold.

Assuming the acquisition is not a hostile takeover, you could factor the costs and time into the offer price.

8.5.3 ACQUIRE OR NOT?

Taking the potential acquisition of the candidate company a step further, you may find enough IT accessibility problems that the acquisition no longer makes business sense for a number of reasons:

- Expense of resolving the accessibility issues
- Time-to-market delays that affect your bottom line
- Risks (IT accessibility–related complaints/litigation) due to integrating or bundling the acquisition's inaccessible components and products with accessible products

8.5.4 TECHNICAL ASSESSMENTS FOR IT ACCESSIBILITY

Including IT accessibility in the acquisition process will require investigation by accessibility experts. Depending on the portfolio of the components and products held by the candidate acquisition company, assessments may be necessary at several levels:

- Assessment of product architecture, development platforms, and programming languages for accessibility enablement viability
- Impact to the accessibility of your organization's solution stacks when acquired products or components are integrated
- Detailing estimated costs of enabling for accessibility offerings
- Performing manual testing (using a screen reader and the like) to determine the accessibility status of major products
- Estimating costs (by order of magnitude) for remediating
- Using code reviews and manual tests (as appropriate) to determine accessibility status of the components planned for integration
- Identifying and documenting issues

8.5.5 **ACQUISITION OF INTERNAL IT**

In the course of performing your due diligence, don't overlook the accessibility of the candidate company's internal IT environment and its employees with disabilities. Whether your organization chooses to migrate the acquisition company's IT to your environment or keep it separate, accessibility-related issues could be lurking.

The following is highly recommended:

- Your organization gain an understanding of the candidate company's internal IT accessibility status for applications and websites with large user populations (e.g., HR self-service)
- You engage your organization's human relations department to work with the candidate company's HR team to understand any known IT-related issues with regard to employees with disabilities

8.6 **IT ACCESSIBILITY EDUCATION AND TRAINING**

The organizational and technical enablement of IT accessibility is not possible unless those responsible for producing IT products have the requisite knowledge and technical training they need. Therefore, an overall IT accessibility-training program should be developed at organizational or unit levels that addresses this topic in ways that are appropriate to employees' roles and responsibilities. The program should reach a broad population of employees and should be developed collaboratively with the accessibility focal points or coordinators, lead developers, and areas of organizational management to ensure that the list of training courses is comprehensive and that all employee roles have been identified.

The matrix that follows is a high-level example of a role-based and needs-based IT accessibility plan.

Example of a role-based IT accessibility training plan

Course level	Course title	General population	State office	Web content producers	Web & application testers	Web application developers	Procurement staff	Contract writers	Contract compliance	Project managers
Fundamentals	Introduction to accessibility (self)	required	required	required	required	required	required	required	required	required
Fundamentals	Office documents (internal)	optional	required	required	optional	optional	required	required	optional	required
Fundamentals	pdf (internal)		required/optional*	required	optional	optional				
Fundamentals	html (internal or external)			required	required	required				
Fundamentals	html forms (internal or external)			required	optional	required				
Fundamentals	testing & tools (internal or external)			required	required	required				
Fundamentals	CSS (internal or external)			optional	optional	required				
Fundamentals	Javascript (internal or external)			optional	optional	required				
Advanced	Dreamweaver (internal or external)					required/optional*				
Advanced	ASP/ASP.net (internal or external)					required/optional*				
Advanced	Java/JSP (internal or external)					required/optional*				
Advanced	web 2.0 technologies (internal or external)					required/optional*				
Specialized	accessibility law, and its impacts						required	required	required	required
Specialized	accessibility in Contract solicitations						required	required	required	required
Specialized	understanding/validating vendor IT accessibility						required	required	required	required

Depending on the status of your organization's IT accessibility journey, the content for some of the training may already exist in internal or external resources. Content for some of the more specialized training may need to be developed internally or even jointly with an external supplier (a fitting task for the centralized IT accessibility organization). Here are some initial steps your organization should take:

- Identify gaps in needed training

- Inventory the IT accessibility courses already in use
- Evaluate the courses for continued use
- Prioritize the development and procurement of new training

8.6.1 DEVELOPMENT AND DELIVERY OF TRAINING

Before developing the content for new courses, your organization needs to determine how it will provide the courses to employees. The main criteria to consider for are the size and geographic location of the population to be trained and the degree of difficulty in each topic area.

If your organization has an employee training department, its staff should be able to analyze the topics and help make recommend delivery methods. Remember, all training and the supporting infrastructure (enrollment tools, course catalogs, etc.) need to be accessible.

8.6.2 WEB-BASED SELF-SERVICE TRAINING

For large user populations, web-based self-service training is an efficient, cost-effective method of delivering entry-level IT accessibility training. Course materials can be developed in simple formats, such as web pages or popular document formats. They can be designed as interactive courses that include video clips (with captions), links to reference content, and integrated testing of course knowledge at various points in the training. Other advantages of web-based, self-service delivery include flexibility in enrollment and course delivery and integration into HR, or systems that track training and reporting.

8.6.3 WEB-BASED INSTRUCTOR-LED TRAINING

For intermediate-level training of a large user population, the information to be conveyed may not be suited to self-service. In such cases, it may be possible to use web conference technologies or a combination of web viewing and telephone conferencing to deliver live instructor-led training to large numbers of users. This approach can also be efficient and cost-effective for high-volume delivery and accommodates questions during or after the session.

Another advantage to this approach is that training sessions can be recorded and posted on the web for reference or even substituted for live instruction. If used in this manner, it's helpful for an instructor to join the conference, at least at the end, to address questions not addressed in the original recording.

8.6.4 CLASSROOM INSTRUCTOR–LED TRAINING

For other intermediate, advanced, and specialized IT accessibility training, or training that requires hands-on use of tools and applications, classroom-based instruction with qualified instructors is the better approach.

Depending on the skills and classroom space within your organization, some of these courses may be taught by internal IT accessibility experts. In other cases, particularly when internal experts are not available, the organization will need to hire instructors.

When working with more advanced or specialized topics, it can be helpful to nominate early graduates of the new coursework to train others who require skills training. This "train the trainers" approach reduces the cost of external training through knowledge transfer.

If an organization has technical certification programs, it may wish to develop a curriculum for an "IT accessibility certification" that identifies the go-to leaders for the most technically challenging accessibility problems.

8.7 THE WEB: INTERNET AND INTRANET

The Internet and intranet are probably the most important elements and most versatile utilities in your organization's possession. Think of each as a multifunction tool, sort of like a Swiss Army knife.

The tools contained within your organization's Internet pages range from product and services information to organizational information, e-commerce, forms, how-to information—you name it. There are thousands, even millions, of pages and many applications to manage.

The same goes for your organization's intranet, except that the information available is much greater, as the intranet may contain more content and more applications than its Internet counterpart. I have discussed the use of web scanning for IT accessibility as a way to track and remediate IT accessibility problems on live sites. But how do these accessibility errors arise to begin with?

Lots of ways. Sometimes they can be attributed to legacy pages and applications published before accessibility was considered. Beyond that, many causes are human based (deliberate and unintentional), as I have discussed.

This is where content management systems (CMS) come into play. Integrating IT accessibility parameters or tools into your organization's CMS allows for the identification of accessibility errors before publishing.

8.7.1 ACCESSIBILITY-INTEGRATED CMS

Accessibility-integrated CMS not only saves the time and expense of post-publication remediation, but it also mitigates the risks associated with publishing inaccessible new content and applications. There are three fundamental ways to integrate accessibility-checking criteria into a CMS. Each is dependent on the features and functions of the CMS an organization uses.

8.7.2 CMS WITH INTEGRATED ACCESSIBILITY CHECKING

Quite simply, CMS with integrated accessibility checking means an accessibility checker is built into the application. It may be offered as a basic function or as an add-on feature. This allows accessibility checking to be done directly within the CMS workflow. When considering an investment in CMS with integrated accessibility checking, be sure you understand the accessibility rule sets that are available for the CMS to ensure that they map (or can be mapped) to the criteria and standards (WCAG 2.0, etc.) that your organization uses.

I mention the rule sets because different checking tools can yield different results based on what or how they perform their checking function. Therefore, the accessibility-checking rules used in the CMS checking function should be consistent with the rules that the organization's accessibility scan tools use for the live web sites. If the results of these two checkers are not consistent, the consequence can be a lot of confusion and inefficient reconciliation of the differences.

Even syntax differences for the same rule can be a problem. Case in point: "skip to main content" navigation. Accessibility requires a link at the top of every web page that, when clicked, allows the user to navigate directly to the main content of the page, bypassing navigation bars. This is an important feature for blind users. When the CMS checker performs its check for that rule, it may look specifically for a link labeled "skip to main content" at the top of every page (it should be there if the site uses cascading style sheets, or CSS). The checker will give a passing grade to all pages that contain a "skip to main content" label and a link. The pages go live, and everyone is happy until a scan tool checks the new, live pages for the first time. The scan tool fails all these new pages because it cannot find the skip links. Why not? Didn't the developers put them in, and didn't they pass the CMS check?

As it turns out, the scan tool is configured to look for a link at the top of every page labeled "navigate to main content," so it fails every new page with "skip to main content."

This is a simple example of why rule customization is important. Synchronize the criteria and rules, and you'll get consistent results, reduce failure, save analysis time and expense, and avoid confusion.

8.7.3 CMS WITH INTEROPERATING ACCESSIBILITY CHECKING

In this approach, the accessibility checking is integrated into the CMS workflow but performed by a checking tool outside the CMS application. The CMS manages and automates the checking process by sending the code to an automated accessibility-checking tool. The tool runs and returns the results to the CMS, and the CMS takes whatever action is needed based on the CMS workflow: it allows pages to be published or rejects them.

The advantage of this approach is that it's possible to use the same accessibility-checking tool for pre-publishing and live web pages, eliminating the synchronization problem described in the previous section.

8.7.4 CMS WITH NO ACCESSIBILITY CHECKING MECHANISM

A CMS of this type means your organization must use some sort of manual process to check IT accessibility. While this approach does not seem to be as state-of-the-art as the other approaches I have mentioned, it has some advantages.

Assuming that qualified testers are available, that the testing is performed downstream of the content or page developer, and that quality checking tools are used (including screen readers), manual testing allows for more complete testing than automated tools can conduct. As I have noted, automated tools such as web scan tools are not able to check against all accessibility criteria and standards.

8.7.5 WEB-BASED COLLABORATION TOOLS

For most of us, the days of getting on a plane to attend a meeting, class, or informational gathering are long past. The Internet and IT have changed this paradigm forever. Today, a staggering number of IT tools and solutions are available that bring people together in virtual ways unimaginable a decade ago. And even more amazing things are on the way.

Although much improved over the past few years, some of these tools may not be enabled for IT accessibility. Excluding your organization's (or customer's) employees with disabilities from participating in these communications and collaborations can be a serious issue. (These employees, by the way, may benefit the most from these methods.) Therefore special care is needed when organizations make decisions about the development, procurement, or use of such products and services, including the following:

- Web conferencing (audio, visual, or both)
- Social media/networking
- Messengers and chat
- Virtual worlds
- Mobile applications

The good news is that accessibility-enabled products and services in this realm are commercially available. Your organization (perhaps with the help of HR) may need to determine the pros, cons, and trade-offs associated with selection and use of this class of web-based products.

8.8 USABILITY FOR PEOPLE WITH DISABILITIES

Usability for people with disabilities is simply the application of usability and user-centered design concepts and principles to IT accessibility.

My hope is that you are already familiar with this area of usability. If not, some people in your organization probably are, and trying to explain it in any depth within the scope of this book would be a disservice to the profession. (A web search of usability will keep you busy for a few hours.)

Usability is a mature field that deals with the human aspects of using a product, service, or task. It's an integral part of the development process at various phases for any project worth undertaking, and it deals several questions:

- Is the product easy to learn?
- Is the interface intuitive?
- Can tasks be completed quickly and efficiently?
- Does the product or task leave the user satisfied?

If you've ever had a bad experience using a product, bad usability almost certainly was a significant part of the problem. Conversely, I'm sure you have used a web application or software product that was a complete pleasure—simple, easy, and quick. You can be sure that someone in usability was involved in making that experience enjoyable.

In terms of usability for people with disabilities, let's say that your organization has just designed a new self-service web application. The development team worked hard and met all the accessibility criteria specified by your organization. The application passed with flying colors all the tests for use by the general population. The application was deployed, but shortly afterward came a flurry of complaints from users with disabilities that the application was not accessible.

What went wrong? As it turned out, usability was designed for the general population, but usability criteria for people with disabilities were not really integrated. Even though the coding was done to accessibility standards, blind users could not complete the task in any reasonable amount of time, complete it correctly, or could not complete it at all. The application met the criteria specified, but people with disabilities couldn't use it.

The goal of usability for people with disabilities in IT accessibility is to ensure that everyone can perform the same IT tasks with the same amount of success, efficiency, and satisfaction.

8.8.1 GATHERING USABILITY REQUIREMENTS FOR ACCESSIBILITY

For almost any development or IT project, user requirements are collected in the initial phases. Many techniques are used to compile these requirements: competitive analysis, user surveys, focus groups, and customer support data are but a few. You may use all these techniques or just a few, depending on budgets, priorities, and other considerations. However, capturing user requirements for people with disabilities is seldom given consideration, though it certainly should be. As mentioned earlier, meeting standard accessibility criteria may still result in IT that people with disabilities cannot use.

It can be challenging to find people with disabilities who can make suggestions as your organization collects requirements for its IT project, and the more specialized the IT product or service is, the smaller the potential pool of users with disabilities you can call on for assistance. Some organizations rely on their own employees with disabilities. Sometimes, schools for people with disabilities can be a resource for obtaining user feedback. Usability or accessibility consultants in the field of IT product development may have built databases of users with disabilities they can call on.

However you choose to do it, be sure from the start to collect and include the requirements of users with disabilities. As I stated earlier, if something isn't in the requirements to begin with, there's almost no chance it will make it into the finished product.

There is a saying within the disability community: "Nothing for us without us." The idea there is to be sure that people with disabilities are part of the development or procurement of IT where accessibility is required (pretty much all IT today!)

8.8.2 USABILITY FOR ACCESSIBILITY DESIGN OBJECTIVES

With the data collected from users with disabilities and analyzed along with all the other user data, you are ready to define your usability design objectives and insert them into the design process. Usability design objectives based on user input may be broad or specific. Here are a few examples:

- Menu organization and design
- Ease of navigation
- Logic and structure of panels or pages
- Time to complete a task
- Number of task completions versus failures
- Number of keystrokes and mouse clicks to complete a task
- Satisfaction ratings

While these examples may appear difficult to quantify, usability professionals can do that; they have techniques for evaluating designs for usability even before the delivery of working products or codes.

Usability for people with disabilities is defined and measured with objectives and evaluation methods similar to those for general usability, because people with disabilities perform the same tasks as everyone else. The success criteria for tasks performed by users with disabilities may be or may not need to be different from those for other users, but the user interface must be designed in a way that accommodates all users in effectively and efficiently.

8.8.3 USABILITY TESTING FOR PEOPLE WITH DISABILITIES

Like all user testing, usability testing for people with disabilities is where the rubber meets road. It should be included in the planning and execution of any usability testing. In a perfect world, users with disabilities as well as other users would perform usability testing. However, as I discussed earlier, finding and recruiting users with disabilities with the required knowledge can be challenging.

But even including one or two can provide valuable data to help determine levels of usability for this population. When using people with disabilities in user testing, it's important to consider the test environment and whether remote testing is appropriate. Bear in mind that the assistive technologies (such as screen readers) used by people with disabilities will be installed on their personal machines and are highly customized to their needs. As a result, allowing people with disabilities to use their own equipment in testing will provide truer results than if they were to use a generic test machine.

8.8.3.1 COMPARATIVE TESTING

Assuming you are able include people with disabilities in usability testing, you may need to develop targets or windows to determine the level of usable accessibility in the IT being tested. If people with disabilities are asked to perform the same tasks as other test subjects, test results will be analyzed for differences between the two groups. For example, did it take longer for a person with a disability to complete a task than it did other users? If not, the IT unit has passed at least one facet of usability testing. If it did take the person with a disability longer to complete a task, how much longer? Is the difference acceptable given the complexity of the task? What needs to be done to improve the usability of the IT unit for people with disabilities?

8.8.4 WHEN PEOPLE WITH DISABILITIES ARE NOT AVAILABLE FOR TESTING

When people with disabilities are not available for usability testing, alternative techniques may be used. Two examples are heuristic evaluation (a form of usability inspection in which usability specialists judge whether each element of a user interface follows a list of established usability criteria) and simulations of how a person with a disability would interact with a product. The major drawback of these alternatives is that they cannot emulate the cognitive processes or other unique characteristics of people with disabilities, so the results won't be as accurate as testing by people with disabilities. Any usability testing that represents people with disabilities testing is better than none at all, but there is no substitute for the real deal.

8.8.5 **BENEFITS FOR ALL**

As I discussed in chapter 3, integration of IT accessibility can, in many cases, enhance the user experience for everyone, not just people with disabilities. Blind people or people with highly impaired vision don't have the benefit of visual reference when they encounter a page or screen, and they rely on screen readers to give them verbal information to navigate the interface. Ambiguous form-field labels, long menu drop-down lists, and subtle event messages are significant impediments for the blind, but these can also be confusing and cumbersome for all users. Such usability issues might not be flagged during usability testing of sighted subjects but will be picked up in usability testing with people with disabilities. This alone is a compelling reason to use testers with disabilities and include people with disabilities in the other phases of development described in this section.

CHAPTER 9

PUTTING IT ALL TOGETHER

Now that you have a reasonable understanding of the elements of organizational enablement of IT accessibility, you will need to create, socialize, and implement strategies and work plans throughout the organization. In hierarchical order, the task may look something like this:

> Accessibility policy
>> Accessibility strategy
>>> Accessibility framework
>>>> Accessibility work plan
>>>>> Accessibility project plans

This structure may be familiar, as it is really just classic project-management waterfall. However, it should be noted that project managers should be well versed aspects of IT accessibility enablement. It's best that project managers engage in the project in their traditional project management roles, focusing on keeping the program organized (including IT accessibility criteria) and on track while allowing IT accessibility experts and consultants to tackle the meat of the project.

9.1 **THE IT ACCESSIBILITY STRATEGY**

A good accessibility strategy must be overarching and holistic and, therefore, should be designed by those with a broad understanding of IT accessibility. Appropriate candidates for authorship may include accessibility experts, other professionals with the requisite level of accessibility knowledge, or even external consultants.

Various approaches exist to developing strategy or other documents for guiding organization-wide IT accessibility. Engaging the participation and suggestions of stakeholders is one such approach, but because they may have limited knowledge and understanding of IT accessibility, this approach may not be efficient or fruitful.

I'm a big proponent of a slightly different approach: developing the initial strategy with a highly knowledgeable small group, which can create it smartly, objectively, and independently. The advantage of this approach is that it can be done without getting bogged down in the details, issues, or agendas of individual stakeholders that may influence the overall strategy significantly and result in a confused, ineffective, or parochial strategy. A draft strategy created in this way can be brought to stakeholders for review, recommendations, and feedback. Not only does this approach result in a faster development cycle, but it also lends itself to a more structured framework for review and recommendations from stakeholders.

Every organization designs and documents its strategy differently. A strategy can be expressed in PowerPoint charts, a long and detailed document, or anything in between. An organization's IT accessibility strategy should have a few key elements:

- An explanation of the need for an IT accessibility program
- A description of the role of accessibility in the organization's primary business or service strategies
- Support for the organization's IT accessibility policy and relevant standards, regulations, and policies

- Definitions of the business objectives for having high-level IT accessibility
- Definitions of assumptions and dependencies
- Definitions of high-level organizational and governance models
- Definitions of high-level funding models or other broad financial information
- The strategic framework for developing operational work plans

9.2 IT ACCESSIBILITY IMPLEMENTATION FRAMEWORKS AND WORK PLANS

It's one thing to gain concurrence for a strategy you have developed, but strategy without an implementation plan is meaningless. So before you pat yourself on the back for a job well done, you have to figure out, using the strategy as a guide, what actually needs to be done to enable the organization for IT accessibility.

Earlier, I mentioned a strategic framework. What follows is an example of a strategic framework for enabling an organization to become IT accessible. This example was developed for a government agency. The left-hand column defines the key program imperatives, and the right-hand column lists high-level actions and focus areas that, when implemented, meet the imperatives.

First, a set of high-level strategic components:

Implementation Components

| Plan Strategically | Automate for productivity and quality | Validate thoroughly, early, and often | Grow awareness and provide education / training | Measure and track progress |

Fig. 12. Accessibility implementation main components

From each of the implementation components, a set of framework imperatives can be defined:

Plan strategically	1. Obtain initiative support of organization executive team 2. Develop long-term organization goals 3. Integrate into or develop processes to ensure consistency over time 4. Select appropriate IT technologies/suppliers 5. Effectively manage the IT accessibility exception process 6. Maintain flexibility to adapt to criteria changes (508 refresh, WCAG 2.0, etc.) 7. Charter a workgroup with representation from key areas of the organization
Automate for productivity and quality	1. Provide developers tools to facilitate and remediate accessibility compliance 2. Integrate accessibility into content management systems/processes 3. Utilize standardized accessible templates (CSS, etc) 4. Ensure browser-neutral accessibility 5. Utilize enterprise-level scan tools for issue identification/resolution
Validate thoroughly, early, and often	1. Test internally developed pages and applications 2. Obtain test documentation and sniff test externally hosted services 3. Test Published documents/information 4. Perform analysis of vendor VPATs and follow up to obtain accurate vendor document to validate 5. Develop or integrate corrective actions process management/tools
Grow awareness and provide education/training	1. Evangelize accessibility throughout organization/IT supplier community 2. Build/maintain organization's technical capacity with SMEs 3. Identify skill gaps, and resolve via and training staffing plans
Measure and track progress	1. Develop goal-appropriate metrics and reporting tools/methods 2. Communicate and utilize results to drive initiative trajectory 3. Maintain processes and results for "audit readiness" posture

Table 9.1

Once you have a framework established, defining the more specific work areas of program implementation becomes much more straightforward and less abstract.

9.3 **THE IT ACCESSIBILITY WORK PLAN**

Using a framework as a guide, you can use the high-level actions (right-hand column above) to develop more detailed work plans and detailed project plans. The examples that follow illustrate the next level of detail for one of the imperatives in the right-hand column of the framework in the example for the government agency. This is where project management starts to play a more important role in the program, because the elements defined in the work plan should be tracked and managed.

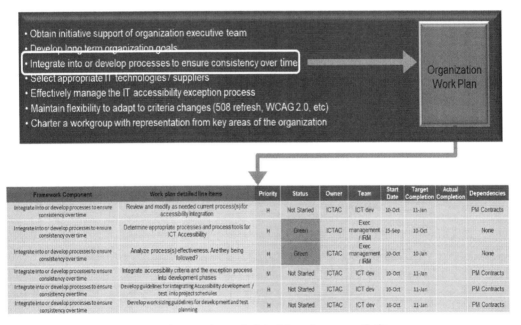

Fig. 13. Second- and third-level accessibility
implementation plan details

Once all the line items in the work plan are defined, project management can assume a more important role by working with line item owners and teams to flesh out the work associated with each. From there, it is classic project management work: break down the structures, sizing, schedules, and other specific program elements so progress can be tracked and managed appropriately.

9.4 PROJECT PLAN DYNAMICS AND FLEXIBILITY

One last piece of advice regarding the development and implementation of IT accessibility enablement initiatives: the IT industry is in a constant state of change, so it's important that IT accessibility work plans are not designed or assumed to be static. They must remain flexible to adapt to new or emerging conditions, whether in the marketplace or within the organization. Given these dynamics, it is recommended that plans be revisited regularly to reassess priority levels and adjust the trajectory. Check for changes in the following areas:

- Marketplace
- Standards, regulations, and policies
- Organizational budgets and resources
- Business strategy
- Technology
- Other business-related factors

Remember that changes to your plan can affect IT accessibility or related work being done in the stakeholder organizations, so you must alert stakeholders to the concept of a "living plan" early in the program and update them when changes that affect them are made.

9.5 WORK PRIORITIZATION

As things get kicked off in your organization, one of the first tasks to consider is how to prioritize the work effort for bringing your organization's IT into compliance with IT accessibility standards. While not a trivial exercise, there are two basic approaches to figuring this out based on your business strategy or other factors. Both are prioritizations based on risk.

9.5.1 **REVENUE-BASED PRIORITIZATION**

Many organizations are now more aware of the legal risks associated with inaccessible IT. For a commercial enterprise that develops IT products or services sold in markets where IT accessibility is required/desired, one can say that shortcomings in IT accessibility can represent a potential risk to an organization's revenue in those markets. That's because purchasing inaccessible products/services can result in legal issues for the purchasing entity if there are people with disabilities that use these products, either as employees or among the general public. Most organizations would prefer to steer clear of such issues for reasons described early in the book and would therefore prefer to buy accessible IT.

If a competitor's products are more accessible than your company's offerings, there is a potential for the customer to select your competitor, assuming that that the customer understands the risks/rewards of accessible products and services, and that the products are generally equivalent in performance and price.

The deference to legal issues by the customer creates a revenue risk to the offering organization if their products are inaccessible.

Therefore, a revenue-based prioritization might look at which products/services are key revenue producers for the company to understand which offerings should be the focus of accessibility and in what timeframe. Such an approach would maximize the benefit of IT accessibility investments.

Depending on how such a prioritization shakes out, an organization might find that the offerings that produce the highest revenues are also the most complex to make accessible. In this case, it may be determined that a slower investment curve to remediate the offering is risky but acceptable. On the other hand, you may forego remediation and wait for the place in the product roadmap where the product is planned for a "grounds up" redo. In these cases, other offerings may be selected for priority IT accessibility work.

It's important to bear in mind that some customers might not yet understand the need for IT accessibility (sadly true, even today). Once your efforts are underway, make sure your marketing/sales teams are aware of IT accessibility features/compliance so they can leverage this information as a sales tool and a differentiator when possible.

9.5.2 USER POPULATION–BASED PRIORITIZATION

The second approach is based on user populations. This involves understanding each piece of IT with respect to the following:

- The purpose of the product/service
- The number of users that regularly interact with it
- Its use by customers/general public.
- Its use internally by an organization, and to what extent.

Typically, a very high user population means there would be higher likelihood of people with disabilities interacting with the IT, and therefore might be viewed as the highest risk.

Conversely, an internal application used by a very low number of users within the organization might be previewed as very low risk and therefore a low propriety in the remediation queue. That said, it's important also to keep in mind that the risk can increase dramatically and quickly—if, let's say, a key employee who uses one of these low-priority, low-user-population applications suddenly loses his vision or a new hire with a disability hires in for a job using that application. Please refer to scenario 6 in previous chapter.

9.5.3 HYBRID REVENUE/RISK-BASED PRIORITIZATION

Although I mentioned only two prioritization approaches, there is, of course, a third, which consists of a combination of a revenue-based and user population–based approach.

Below is an example of such a prioritization hierarchy that contains both elements. The prioritization is depicted as an upside-down pyramid with external offerings depicted in the top section of the pyramid, and internal IT represented on the bottom sections. Note that both revenue and user populations are included in a logical fashion for this example (i.e., high number of external users equals high revenue, a low number of internal users, and no revenue); however, in reality, these relationships between revenue/user populations or internal low# of users/low risk may not be that simple. Data and critical thinking required!

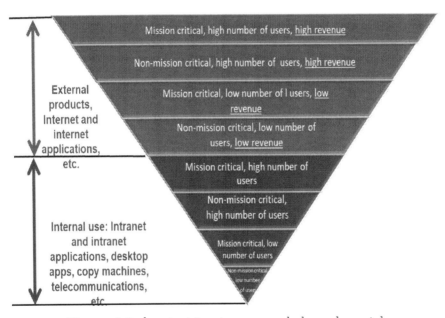

Fig. 14. Work prioritization example based on risk

CHAPTER 10

WORKPLACE MANAGEMENT FOR EMPLOYEES WITH DISABILITIES

Most of this book has discussed the business end of IT accessibility: justifications, integration, strategy, and so on. IT accessibility is not just about putting processes, staff, and other resources in place to comply with IT accessibility standards, regulations, and policies. It is more than a large, abstract business challenge. It's about people.

Because IT accessibility is so broad and complex, it can be easy to lose sight of the prime directive (for you *Star Trek* fans) of IT accessibility: enabling all people to use and access IT.

Admittedly, given all that development and IT managers have on their plates at any given time, focusing on accessibility compliance and not thinking about the underlying human side of why IT accessibility is needed may be an occupational hazard. From the manager's perspective, IT accessibility is like any other project: requirements to satisfy, standards to comply with, and specific criteria to meet. Some managers may understand the human aspect more than others, especially if they have loved ones or friends and neighbors with disabilities and see firsthand the struggles they deal with daily.

But for human resources professionals especially, IT accessibility cannot be viewed in the abstract. The human resources department is responsible and accountable for the well-being of all employees. One can argue that HR's responsibility and accountability for IT accessibility does not stop at current employees. What about potential employees? Or retired employees?

10.1 IT ACCESSIBILITY CONSIDERATIONS FOR EMPLOYEES WITH DISABILITIES

In the introduction, I discussed how people with disabilities in today's workforce are uniquely dependent on accessible IT technology. This characteristic differentiates them from all other diversity groups and users of technology.

The responsibility to ensure that no barriers exist in the recruiting and employment of people with disabilities rests squarely on the shoulders of the human resources organization. What does this mean from an IT perspective? Broadly, this means that HR management must develop, maintain, and enforce procedures and policies related to the use of an organization's IT that prevent discrimination against present, past, or future employees with disabilities and that enable them to do their jobs.

Operationally, this has several implications:

1. IT-based recruiting and hiring tools must be accessible and usable by people with disabilities, maintain the privacy of candidate information, and not require candidates to disclose their disability (disclosure laws vary from nation to nation).
2. Training, processes, and procedures for managers within the organization should

- articulate the importance and benefits of employing people with disabilities;
- provide HR tools and resources for recruiting, managing, and developing people with disabilities; and
- provide information, guidance, and support for assessing and obtaining accommodations for employees with disabilities.

3. Self-service HR tools and other tools used by employees that contain or use personal information must be fully accessible.
4. IT used in the performance of job duties must be accessible, or appropriate accommodations must be made that allow parity in productivity with other employees.
5. Procedures and processes must be in place for assessing the need for special accommodations for employees on an as-needed or as-requested basis.

If your organization has diversity programs, implementation plans that address these operational-level requirements for people with disabilities demand serious consideration.

10.2 IT ACCOMMODATIONS FOR PEOPLE WITH DISABILITIES

As I have discussed, people with disabilities are a unique group of employees because the IT technology they use must be enabled for accessibility. But another way to think about enablement for accessibility is that the IT must interoperate with the hardware and software tools used by people with disabilities. Assistive technology is a bridge between the human and the IT interface. Without assistive technologies, it would be impossible for many people with disabilities to use IT. Several or many assistive technologies may be available for any given disability that can form this crucial bridge.

Here are some examples, mapped according to disability type.

Disability	assistive technology examples
Blind	Screen readers, Braille displays, optical character-recognition devices
Low vision	Screen magnifiers, screen readers, font and color customizations
Deaf	Voice-recognition tools (speech to text), automatic captioning, sign-language conversion tools
Hearing impairment	Sound amplification tools, voice recognition tools, automatic captioning
Mobility impairment	Mouth sticks, head trackers, voice recognition tools (speech to text), oversize keyboards, sticky keys, etc.
Cognitive impairment	Learning software, specialized tools

Table 9.2

For each type of assistive technology, there can be multiple manufacturers or products, each with its own features, characteristics, and price.

To understand and best accommodate a person with a disability, each person with a disability must be viewed as unique. This requires an accommodations program or process that satisfies the following criteria:

- Provides individual assessments by qualified health professionals
- Allows individuals with disabilities to evaluate assistive technology accommodations as part of the accommodation selection process (this may include the assistive technologies requested by people with disabilities)
- Is minimally constrained by budget considerations

- Includes assistance with installation and training
- Monitors progress periodically
- Keeps abreast of new products and enhancements on the market
- Permits trials of new solutions if current ones do not work well

10.3 **SUPPORT INFRASTRUCTURE FOR PEOPLE WITH DISABILITIES AND THEIR MANAGERS**

People with disabilities are often at a disadvantage when it comes to hiring opportunities and career advancement. In an effort to offset or mitigate this problem, many organizations (and even countries) develop hiring programs that communicate the importance and advantages of hiring people with disabilities. This can even include public service advertising campaigns about hiring people with disabilities.

It's not that managers are intentionally discriminatory in their staffing practices; they may just be wary of the incremental or unknown effort that may be required to manage people with disabilities. However, if an organization has appropriate management training, efficient processes, and support tools in place that address the unique needs of both people with disabilities and their managers, much of that "additional effort" is eliminated. There now many public sector and nonprofit organizations who are actively working in a variety of ways to assist employers in addressing all of the dimensions of the employee life cycle for people with disabilities. In the United States, the Office of Disability Employment Policy (ODEP) and the Partnership on Employment & Accessible Technology (PEAT) are two examples of such organizations, but there are many others at local, state, and national level.

Providing these services to both management and employees requires an integrated combination of manual and automated processes that include the following:

- Self-service requests by employees with disabilities for accommodations
- Accessible recruiting tools for job candidates, HR, and hiring managers
- Training for managers about the accommodations process
- Training for managers on workplace issues for people with disabilities
- Assessment processes for workplace accommodations for employees with disabilities
- Purchasing assistive technology or other accommodations
- Accessible, online collaborative and information resources for employees and managers

Of course, everything must be accessible, as you may have already guessed.

10.4 MANAGING IT ACCESSIBILITY ISSUES FOR PEOPLE WITH DISABILITIES

With or without good processes and procedures for dealing with people with disability issues, workplace issues will arise that are related to IT for people with disabilities. As good HR professionals will tell you, any problem brought forth by an employee with a disability should be taken seriously and resolved with care, sensitivity, and respect for the individual.

Sometimes the manager and the employee can resolve IT accessibility issues themselves. Sometimes resolution can be obtained through the involvement of multiple stakeholder areas of the organization. Handling issues of people with disabilities well can make the difference between a loyal, productive, happy employee and a discrimination lawsuit. Here are a few helpful guidelines for managers in dealing with such issues:

- Take immediate action the first time an issue comes up.

- Meet with the employee to discuss and understand as much as possible about the specific problem, and maintain good communications throughout the process.
- Communicate with and engage the human resource staff for support and guidance.
- Engage other areas as needed. These might include

  o Accessibility experts
  o Internal IT development
  o Purchasing
  o Legal counsel
  o Medical staff or other occupational workplace services
  o External services

- Consider the employee's recommendations, suggestions, and ideas about how to resolve the issue when possible.
- When multiple potential solutions or products are found, work closely with the employee to find the best fit.
- Ensure that potential solutions are not dismissed because of cost.
- Ensure that the solution selected is reasonable and does not unduly burden either the employee or the organization.
- Maintain accurate and appropriate documentation throughout the process.
- Develop contingency plans with HR and other areas in case a workable accommodation cannot be found.

CHAPTER 11 | MAINTAINING MOMENTUM

L et's assume that your IT accessibility program is moving ahead nicely. Most of the major work for enabling the organization is complete. Substantial investments in commitment, time, and resources have been made to make the program operational. Key initialization elements of the program have been implemented, and teams are still working their way through the prioritized work plans. All this has resulted in your organization's making strong progress in delivering accessible IT for many of its projects. Great job! But are you done? What do you need to do to ensure the long-term viability, success, and return on your organization's investment in IT accessibility initiatives?

11.1 IMPORTANT CONSIDERATIONS FOR THE ONGOING JOURNEY

IT accessibility enablement, both organizationally and technically, is an ongoing journey—and will be for the foreseeable future. It's difficult to predict what levels of effort may be needed over time, as many environmental factors, both external and internal to your organization, will play a role in determining this. Consider these influences:

- As global populations mature, the demand and revenue opportunities for accessible IT will increase significantly.
- Emerging technologies may continue to create future technical challenges for enabling accessibility.
- Emerging technologies will provide potential improvements in enabling IT for accessibility, on both the development side and the assistive technology side.
- Standards, regulations, and policies for IT accessibility will continue to evolve, with varying levels of impact in the public and private sectors.
- Standards, regulations, and policies for IT accessibility will drive improvements in tools, technologies, and services for enabling IT accessibility.
- IT accessibility will become a more important competitive differentiator in the IT industry.
- New areas within your organization will be found where IT accessibility will need to play a role.
- Business priorities will change.

This is not a trivial set of examples. I touched upon some of these topics earlier in the context of developing the overall accessibility program or initiative. Now I need to discuss these factors from more of a "post-enablement" perspective, by looking at the life of the program.

11.2 PERIODIC IT ACCESSIBILITY PROGRAM ASSESSMENTS

With all the time and effort that has been dedicated to putting the organizational enablement in place for IT accessibility, there should be little need for change in the overall program for quite a while, right?

If you look back at the important considerations listed in the previous section, it's clear that periodic adjustments to major elements of the IT accessibility program within the organization will be necessary. Therefore, in addition to measuring and tracking IT accessibility in products, services, or internal IT, periodic assessments of the effectiveness of the overall program should be conducted. Such assessments must look at the program at a more strategic level, including market and technological factors and compliance-level progress for the organization's products, services, and internal IT.

Looking at the program through both lenses could result in changes to the following:

- Organization
- Policy
- Governance
- Investment strategy
- Products, services, and internal IT priorities

11.3 IT ACCESSIBILITY METRICS

Measuring and tracking progress is a fundamental element of an IT accessibility program. At face value, this data will drive accessibility improvements through whatever corrective actions or quality processes are used. However, deeper analysis can indicate problems at a higher level. Results may uncover issues in such areas as developer and testing tools, base technologies, project and personnel management, training gaps, prioritization, and more. Also, a standard may have changed that renders formerly accessible IT inaccessible.

Action plans that address these indirect noncompliance issues (direct issues are actual code errors) are strategic and can result in a dramatic improvement to IT accessibility levels and efficiency when the problems are rectified.

11.4 **PROGRAM VISIBILITY**

Creating and delivering those initial presentations to your organization's executives was stressful, no doubt, but instrumental in gaining their agreement, support, funding, and many other things that allowed the program to go forward. To ensure that IT accessibility remains relevant and on management's radar, maintaining the program's visibility to top management and stakeholders is vital. The folks at the executive level need something a bit more engaging than accessibility metrics and tracking reports. Meeting with executives face-to-face to discuss the overall state of IT accessibility in the industry and organizational environment is an excellent way to accomplish this.

There is also high value in communicating to broader audiences about IT accessibility, not only in relation to activities inside the organization but also concerning items of interest in the marketplace, research and technology, and current events. For example, you might want to address the following:

- Wins by your organization in the marketplace in which IT accessibility played a role
- IT accessibility success stories within the organization
- IT accessibility success stories within the industry
- New science and technology that provide people with disabilities with better tools
- Relevant statistical and research reports from government organizations and nongovernmental organizations
- Any other information that articulates the importance and need for IT accessibility

Using an organization's intranet and Internet capabilities is an excellent method of delivering broader communications; this not only helps reinforce the importance of the message but also promotes the organization's public image and brand. Social media can also be effectively used to share information.

11.5 **MARKET INTELLIGENCE AND COMPETITIVE ANALYSIS**

As I discussed in chapter 3 and in several of the scenarios, IT accessibility levels can make or break purchasing decisions, particularly in markets where accessibility is required by law or there is a business requirement for IT accessibility. If your organization is in the business of developing and marketing products, understanding how you measure up to your competitors in IT accessibility helps ensure that your products and services remain competitive. Therefore, IT accessibility should be included as part of whatever market intelligence and competitive analysis activities are performed by your organization.

Inferior accessibility can translate into high risk and potential loss of revenue. Superior accessibility can produce just the opposite; plus, you can use your superior accessibility in marketing and sales pitches and in other ways that increase equity in your organization's brand. Here are a few methods for evaluating the IT accessibility of your competition:

- Perform VPAT line-item comparisons of your and your competitors' product VPATs. (Remember that VPATs may not be accurate, but they are still better than nothing.)
- Perform Internet research using credible product reviews, blogs, discussion forms, and other sources. Find out what experts and users are saying about your competitors' IT accessibility levels and yours.
- Purchase or obtain competitive products and perform some accessibility testing, including with the use of a screen reader. Then compare these results to test data from your comparable products.
- Perform accessibility testing on your competitors' products or services that are available as internet applications.
- Perform accessibility evaluations on competitors' home pages and a few sample pages or search for their VPATs.

This can give you an idea of their level of knowledge and awareness of accessibility. Poor accessibility on frequently visited pages, and a lack of information on accessibility or VPATs, can be telling.

Keeping abreast of trends, new technologies, and other activities around IT accessibility in the marketplace is also important. This includes monitoring standards, regulations, and policies on IT accessibility that may be changing or emerging in places where your organization does business. Sharing with high-level executives and stakeholders the highlights of market intelligence findings and the competitive landscape can be valuable in keeping IT accessibility visible, relevant, and funded.

11.6 **BUSINESS RESULTS**

How IT accessibility affects revenue is information that executives and stakeholders will be especially interested in. Whether the news is positive or negative, it can be beneficial to the trajectory of the program.

Revenue that can be directly attributed to IT accessibility sends the message that the program is working and that there is a need for continued investment in IT accessibility to stay ahead of the competition.

Lost business that can be directly attributed to IT accessibility can communicate the need for greater investment in the program to ensure competitiveness. In this scenario, executives trying to understand what happened are likely to ask difficult questions of those responsible for problem areas and will want to know what can be done to ensure problems don't recur.

11.7 **PARTICIPATING IN INDUSTRY GROUPS OR ORGANIZATIONS RELATED TO IT ACCESSIBILITY**

Involvement, formal or informal, with nonprofits, industry groups, standards bodies, or other organizations with a focus on IT accessibility is an excellent way to build industry recognition for your organization and establish leadership in IT accessibility. There is quite a diversity of groups operating at the local, regional, industry, national, and international level. These groups deal with every aspect of accessibility imaginable. Gaining membership may be as simple as paying a membership fee; more powerful organizations may require annual contributions from your organization, while some memberships may be by invitation only.

Before joining or committing to any of these bodies, it's wise to inform appropriate levels of management of the plan to participate and to thoroughly research what the organization does and whether its goals and objectives are compatible with those of your organization. In addition to the credibility and reputation boost you can gain, membership also provides

- Opportunities for your organization to contribute to and influence aspects of IT accessibility beyond the walls of your organization
- Information and insight into what's happening in the industry and marketplace that may influence your organization's plans and strategies

11.8 USING AUDIT AND BUSINESS CONTROLS PROCESSES

In chapters 7 and 8, I discussed business audit controls: what they are, why they are needed, implementation considerations, and the stigma they sometimes carry. Nothing says focus and attention like a rigorous audit, right?

While not necessarily welcomed by the leaders and staff of areas being audited, audits are an effective way to drive progress and maintain or increase momentum in IT accessibility. Even in an area that is executing well and showing great results in IT accessibility, the audit will invariably uncover a few small areas for improvement.

Corrective actions in an area that is already doing well will result in even better execution. For areas that are performing poorly, auditors will find an abundance of issues, and many corrective actions will be needed and tracked—driving improvement and moving the ball forward. As you can see, audits aren't all bad. In fact, they are a key ingredient in increasing momentum.

11.9 REACHING THE END OF THE JOURNEY: ACCESSIBILITY NIRVANA

Enabling an organization and all its IT for accessibility is a little like raising a child. A newborn comes into the world totally helpless, requiring the full attention of its parents for care and feeding. While learning to walk, talk, and adapt to the complexities of the environment it lives in, it still requires a lot of parental guidance. As the child matures into adulthood, the need for parental guidance diminishes; the individual is fully self-sustaining, no longer dependent on parental guidance.

Self-sufficiency is the goal for the IT accessibility enablement program, for both organizational and technical enablement. A program can be seen as fully implemented when IT accessibility is so intricately woven into the focus areas and stakeholder organizations that it just becomes part of the organization's everyday operations, requiring no additional consideration, effort, or thought.

At later stages of your journey, you may be able to consider reducing the size of the staff dedicated to accessibility by transferring some employees to other areas of the organization. This approach helps retain and spread specialized IT accessibility skills within the organization. Other dedicated IT accessibility functions may no longer be needed at all, either because they are integrated fully into other areas of the organization or because the work was tactical and was completed.

This level of enablement marks the final leg of your journey toward IT accessibility. Congratulations!

ING
NETHERLANDS
STRATEGIC ACCESSIBILITY

Changing the Culture: The Many IT Accessibility Initiatives for the ING Bank

A Tsunami of Access

Since then, ING has introduced different initiatives to ensure full customer accessibility to their services and products, initially on a somewhat ad-hoc basis. However, in 2006, the United Nations launched its Convention on the Rights of Persons with Disabilities (CRPD). "This created a 'tsunami of access' affecting all big corporates," says Jake Abma, who, alongside being Product Owner for Team A11Y in the Netherlands, is also a UN CRPD Ambassador and member of the W3C WCAG working Group setting the global standard for inclusive ICT.

"The CRPD changed the definitions," Jake explains. "It was no longer the person who had a problem, but the product, service or environment; if it had barriers that hindered a disabled person's full participation in society on an effective and equal basis with others, then it needed changing."

Country Framework

Since then, Jake and his team have been a passionate promoter of accessibility. They set up and made sure that accessibility principles could be found within ING's previous user interface framework called "The Guide". The framework evolved and accessibility is now being strategically placed within a larger global ecosystem. "And it's not just for IT, but for Product Owners, designers, developers, the whole spectrum." The name for the team is Team A11Y. "'A' and 'Y' are the first and last letters of 'accessibility'," Jake explains, and there are 11 characters in between".

Role models

Inspired by companies like the BBC and Barclays Bank, who are at a high level of maturity, he also cites Google, Microsoft, IBM and Facebook as good examples from a business perspective. "Companies like the BBC and Barclays train their employees on accessibility, support external organizations and educational institutes, involve people with disabilities in their processes, support the elderly, give presentations and share their approach with people like us. They've been busy with this for over a decade and we can learn a lot from them."

The search for an own strategic approach was based on models and standards from different makers. Researching the British Standard for Accessibility BS 7888, the accessibility maturity models from Deque and the Business Disability Forum (BDF) the team ended up with a preference for the work of Jeff Kline and the National Association of State CIOs or NASCIO. Jake: "Technically extracting the different dimensions, aspects and artifact for accessibility is not the difficult challenge. Embedding and managing the right approach within the way of work and culture of a specific company is."

Although at the time Team A11Y started ING didn't have a policy specifically for accessibility, the PDAA Governance Model gave a head start as it is "intentionally written to be very broad, leaving it up to the organization to utilize it as best fits an organization and its culture'. Keeping it clear and easy is for the small team essential to make progress on a regular basis without being trapped in a too overwhelming maturity model. The three levels involved, launch, integrate and optimize help tackling the approach. Strategically the decision was made to start with an Accessibility Champion Model in combination with Inclusive Testing for teams.

Inclusive design

Jake points out that while accessibility typically addresses users who have a disability (impaired vision or hearing for example), it has a much broader scope. "It is strictly defined as: 'the technical and usability quality standard of a product, service, environment or facility, for people with the widest range of capabilities'." A term Jake uses a lot is 'inclusive design'. As Microsoft states: "Inclusive principles are a design methodology that enables and draws on the full range of human diversity". "A lot of people use a zoom tool to make text more legible, zooming in up to 400% or more. But if our designers don't take into consideration that what is happening on the right-hand part of the screen, which may not be visible to all our customers when they are zoomed in, then they're not making the right design decisions'.

For the team the direct focus is on accessibility and providing teams training on how to test for inclusive principles for design and development.

For inspiration ING has created an Inclusive Testing approach. It supports for different contexts like: Physical, Social, Temporary/ Situational Limit, Role of Technology, Examples of Mismatch, Conditions and The Persona Spectrum.

Inclusive Testing Example

Testing for inclusiveness is validating your current assumptions on the completeness of how technology should function from different perspectives.

Questioning all interactive elements and content to understand an application and all techniques used, by testing with inclusive principles in mind is the key to improvements.

Start with Inclusive Principles
Be sure to study the equivalent level for Inclusive Principles provided with the testing level. This provides context for performing the test.

Testing Levels
All testing is based on user needs and build towards the 3rd level: "conformance with the global standard for accessibility (WCAG)".

Step 1. Assumptions & Questions
Just look at the requirements, design file or, if already build, the screen **(don't use your mouse, touch, keyboard or assistive technology yet!).**

1A: Analysis
When analyzing an application we're focusing on: important steps to consider, discuss how it should function, self-contained content, everyone perceive information, formulate questions.

1B: Iterate
After fully completing step 1A, continue to the next page, view or state of what you test without validating the content or functionality and iterate over step 1A and step 1B till you're done.

Step 2. Validation Process
Only, and only when you're done iterating over step 1A and 1B, start validating!

2A: Procedures and Results Level

Depending on the situation, need and knowledge, use the explanation, procedures and results from the different Testing Levels. In each phase all validation can be done by all disciplines: CJE, UX, Design and Developers.

2B: Development Life Cycle Phases

Inclusive Testing can be applied at all times for all phases within the Development Life Cycle. Due to the preconditions there's some customization for Requirement, Design or for Build application vase.

2C: Issues found

Unless you have a photographic memory and no one else will ever need the information make sure to write down all issues found.

Inclusive Testing Result

For the new banking environment we've used this method to see where user needs were conflicting with the new technology chosen to build the renewed banking application. The result was we soon found practical but core functionality which needed an update to easily use our pages for all our customers.

Some of the issues found were:

Routing: we use what is called a "single page application" and needed to simulating default page load behavior to make sure all users experienced a page as they are used to when entering the application.

Landmarks: page structure is very important for all people to quickly understand and navigate within pages. For this structure we made some adjustments to make tab focus follow the focus of assistive technology for equal experiences. Also providing accessible names for the landmarks made using the page more usable.

Menu's: using menus in a consistent way for all users we decided to harmonize all implementations and made sure the trigger buttons were clear and conveyed all information for usage, also for people using screen readers. The opening menus are all based on a dialog menu for consistency of experiences to customers so they know when they are interacting with the menu and when they are outside of the meu.

One solution for many people

And there's a huge range of cognitive faculties to take account of too. Jake: "UX guru Nielsen Norman carried out research showing that university graduates and non-native speakers or people with a low IQ both preferred reading content written for a 12-year-old, which shows that one solution can serve a lot of people. Applying that sort of knowledge helps make our decisions inclusive." So that's the usability.

As far as the technology goes, it's crucial that we use the right technology says Jake: "If what appears on the screen is not present in the code, then the site, or app, is not as effective as it could be. A screen reader for example, must be aware that a link is a link, or a header a header."

From a principle perspective an equal experience must be presented to all users and when possible, baked into the same products. User needs are the same all over the world and so establishing an organizational structure where unified core criteria are defined, refined and centrally offered is key to success. When adopted and implemented in the development life cycle processes we're up to a better world.

Champions Model

Building the right technology, creating standards and managing the cultural change is a top priority for the accessibility team. The team itself is made up of people with different disciplines, such as IT, UX, design and product ownership where some people in the team have a disability themselves. The reach on a more personal basis in a very large company is limited though and here the key to success is to come up with the right scalable approach. "We're also setting up a

Champions Network, inspired by BBC and Barclays, in the end they will do the hard work of being the real ambassadors for inclusive products", says Jake.

Role and Responsibility Criteria Accessibility Champions:
An Accessibility Champion is an ambassador for **inclusive principles within squads** and **shares knowledge** within the Accessibility Community.

Inclusive principles within squads
A champion considers and encourages inclusive design and development from the start of the project until the end, for example:

- When defining requirements
- During design and development
- Testing for accessibility
- Share findings
- Offer first-line support
- Refer colleagues to the proper resources and information

Share knowledge
Champions share knowledge and are active within the Accessibility Community, for example:

- Active on internal chat channel
- Join and contribute to meetups
- Attend workshops
- Demo accessibility achievements
- Assist other champions

Accessibility Guild

An Accessibility Guild within ING is another of the A11Y Team initiatives. The Guild, or Accessibility Community invites colleagues from different departments – IT, communication, debit cards, ATMs, branding, to come together, give presentations and see how we can all help and strengthen each other. "This is currently just in the

Netherlands," says Jake, "but with the rise in modular architecture, with global projects in the make, it could become relevant for other countries too." The team is in regular contact with countries such as Spain, Poland, Germany and Belgium, sharing best practices on accessibility from the Netherlands.

We're all familiar with 'anytime, anywhere'. Maybe we should add 'for anyone' to that?

Global Framework

Jake was one of the initiators of a nationwide 'User Interface Framework', set up in conjunction with the ICT department. The framework has evolved over the years into a global framework, which now involves lots of teams in many different countries, sharing best practices on a range of topics and setting the global standard for ING. From within this framework the inclusive principles are now being implicitly secured.

From within the new global organization we 're working on the base criteria and designating champs strategically in teams. Within the development lifecycle the goal is to implicitly secure accessibility in all places where appropriate, make sure the right user manuals are available and having integrated accessibility tests used by all teams.

The awareness for and training of staff is sprinkled across the global framework and processed within an internal global academy.

Inclusive Banking is the future

ING wants to help all customers with digital banking. Also customers for whom it is not so obvious to be able to use our (digital) services. It doesn't matter if they are blind and/or deaf or have another physical or cognitive impairment, older people but also young people. Our vision is that small changes in our products or services can already have a major impact on them, our ambition is to have big changes follow.

REFERENCE INFORMATION

Country Legal Information

Index of country policies   www.w3.org/WAI/Policy/

General Accessibility

Texas Health and Human https://accessibility.hhs.texas.gov/
Services Accessibility Center
California State University www.calstate.edu/accessibility/

General Accessibility—Web

Web Accessibility in Mind http://webaim.org/
World Wide Web Consortium www.w3.org/WAI/
of the Web Accessibility
Initiative

           http://lflegal.com/
           negotiations/ http://lflegal.
Litigation and Settlements com/category// settlements/
           web-accessibilitysettlements/
           www.nfb.org/nfb/Default.asp

NGOs

National Federation of the
Blind

American Foundation for the Blind	http://afb.org/
American Council for the Blind	http://www.acb.org/
Information Technology Industry Council	www.itic.org/
Royal National Institute of Blind People	www.rnib.org.uk/Pages/Home.aspx
Global Initiative for Inclusive Information and Communication Technologies	http://g3ict.org/

Standards, Regulations, and Policies

Section 508 of the Rehabilitation Act of 1973	www.section508.gov/
Americans with Disabilities Act (U.S.)	www.ada.gov/
World Wide Web Consortium	www.w3.org/
International Organization for Standardization, Standard 9241	www.iso.org/iso/home.html

Tools

World Wide Web Consortium of the Web Accessibility Initiative	www.w3.org/WAI/ER/tools/complete.html
Freedom Scientific	www.freedomscientific.com/
Adobe	www.adobe.com/accessibility

| Web Accessibility in Mind | http://webaim.org/ |

| Texas Health and Human Services Accessibility Center | https://accessibility.hhs.texas.gov/ |

Usability

| Jakob Nielsen's Website | www.useit.com/ |

GLOSSARY

Accessibility coordinator—Individual responsible for IT accessibility within an organization.

Accessibility developer tools—IT tools used by software application or web content developers that facilitate the technical enablement of IT accessibility. **Accessibility focal point**—Individual responsible for IT accessibility at a unit or subunit level of an organization.

Accessibility metrics—Goals and measurements that track progress of IT accessibility by an organization.

Accessibility policy—An overarching governance instrument for an organization's IT accessibility initiative.

Accessibility process integration—The integration of IT accessibility criteria into an organization's development and business processes.

Accessible—IT that can be understood and used by individuals with and without disabilities.

Accommodation—Any modification or adjustment to a job or work environment that enables a qualified individual with a disability to apply for a job or an employee with a disability to perform essential job functions. Reasonable accommodation also includes adjustments to ensure that a qualified individual with a disability has rights and privileges in employment equal to those of employees without disabilities.

Acquisition—The purchase of a business or corporation by another business or corporation.

ADA—Americans with Disabilities Act.

Alternate formats—Formats usable by people with disabilities that may include, but are not limited to, Braille, ASCII text, large print, recorded audio, and electronic formats.

Alternate methods—Different means of providing information, including product documentation, to people with disabilities.

Alternate methods may include, but are not limited to, voice, fax, relay service, TTY, Internet posting, captioning, text-to-speech synthesis, and audio description.

Assistive technology—Any item, piece of equipment, or system, whether acquired commercially, modified, or customized, that is commonly used to increase, maintain, or improve functional capabilities of individuals with disabilities.

AT—Assistive technology.

Automated accessibility-checking tools—Specialized software products used to evaluate large numbers of web pages (unassisted) for aspects of IT accessibility, documenting the error type and location.

Buy Accessible Wizard—A web-based application (http://www. buyaccessible. gov) that guides users through a process of gathering data and providing information about electronic and information resources and Section 508 compliance, or other tools and resources developed by or for the federal government to indicate product and service compliance with the Section 508 standards (http://www. section508.gov).

Centralized accessibility—A department or area in an organization that contains appropriate technical resources and is responsible for all key aspects of an organization's accessibility program.

CMS—Content management system.

DDA—Disability Discrimination Act (U.K.).

Executive sponsor—A high-level executive within an organization who helps promote, fund, and champion a particular business activity/initiative.

Heuristic evaluation—A form of usability inspection in which usability specialists judge whether each element of a user interface follows a list of established usability criteria.

HTML—HyperText Markup Language.

Information technology—Any equipment or interconnected system or subsystem of equipment that is used in the automatic acquisition, storage, manipulation, management, movement, control, display, switching, interchange, transmission, or reception of data or information. The term includes computers, ancillary equipment, software, firmware and similar procedures, services (including support services), and related resources.

IT accessibility organizational enablement—The execution of organizational, business, and process activities that weaves IT accessibility into the fabric of the organization's policies, processes, and culture.

IT accessibility technical enablement—The execution of specific technical aspects of enabling IT for access and use by people with disabilities.

Manual accessibility testing tools—Software tools used by developers and content producers to test by manual analysis the accessibility of IT products and services.

MI—Market intelligence: the gathering of direct and implied information in a particular business area or market.

Neutral placement—Providing a location within an organization for a business function that is autonomous and not subject to the business agenda of any particular unit or subunit.

NFB—National Federation for the Blind.

NGO—Nongovernmental organization.

Operable controls—A component of a product that requires physical contact for normal operation. Operable controls include, but are not limited to, mechanically operated controls, input and output trays, card slots, keyboards, and keypads.

Organizational subunit—A subdivision of an organizational unit defined by particular function(s) and management structure.

Organizational unit—An area defined by particular functions and management structure within an organization.

Section 508 compliance—Using testing and validation tools and procedures to check web pages and Internet content for compliance with the Section 508 requirements of the Rehabilitation Act relating to Web accessibility contained in 36 CFR 1194.

Self-contained, closed products—Products that generally have embedded software and are commonly designed so that a user cannot easily attach or install assistive technology. These products include, but are not limited to, information kiosks and information transaction machines, copiers, printers, calculators, fax machines, and other similar products.

Software stack—A set of software subsystems or components needed to deliver a fully functional solution, e.g., a product or service.

SRPs—Standards, regulations, policies.

Technology platform—A development and delivery environment based on a particular technology and its associated tools.

TTY—Teletypewriter: machinery or equipment that uses interactive text-based communications through the transmission of coded signals across the telephone network. TTYs may include, for example, devices known as TDDs (telecommunication display devices or telecommunication devices for deaf persons) or computers with special modems. TTYs are also called text telephones.

Usability—Design criteria that focus on user performance, ease of navigation, visual appeal, and straightforwardness.

Accessible Usability—The application of usability principles and techniques to the evaluation of usability of IT for people with disabilities.

Voluntary Product Accessibility Template (VPAT)—A standardized summary of accessibility information about a product or service, meant to assist contracting officials and other buyers in making preliminary assessments regarding features that support accessibility.

W3C—World Wide Web Consortium. Additional information and copies of the current standards and recommendations are available at http://www.w3.org. **WCAG**—Web Content Accessibility Guidelines, released by the Web

Accessibility Initiative as guidelines for the creation of accessible sites.

Web Accessibility Initiative—A subproject of the World Wide Web Consortium

(W3C) pursuing accessibility of the web.

INDEX

A

accessibility. *See* IT accessibility

accessibility compliance.
    See compliance

accessibility coordinators 59, 94

accessibility development 13, 57, 121, 149

accessibility education 155

accessibility education and training 155

accessibility exceptions 60, 62
    metrics and tracking
        progress 105
    product development and
        78, 114

accessibility framework 169

accessibility initiative 33, 93, 94, 105, 106, 206
    goals and 58, 108, 193

accessibility issues xv, xvii, 15, 16, 25, 30, 38, 44, 52, 60, 62, 85, 86, 90, 130, 138, 146, 147, 154, 184
    inaccurate documentation xii, 90, 103, 136, 141, 145
    lawsuits. (*see* accessibility related lawsuits)
    legal department and 86

accessibility program cost and funding 67, 72, 74
    acquisitions 44, 46, 58, 107, 110, 131, 133
    assessment (metrics and tracking) 4, 47, 65, 88, 102, 137, 141, 142, 152, 153
    exceptions xii, 28, 41, 57, 60, 62, 96, 102, 107, 149
    funding models 70, 71, 73, 171
    training 172

accessibility project office 57

accessibility-related lawsuits 25

accessibility strategy 106, 170

accessibility technology gap 7

accessibility testing 82, 116, 119, 136, 137, 138, 144, 145, 149, 150, 151, 191, 208. *See also* accessibility tools
    architecture and ix, xvi
    funding and 53, 68
    language and 71, 127, 135
    manual testing 74, 104, 154, 161
    procurement and 221

accessibility tools 117
    for developer/facilitation 57, 78, 95
    for tests 149

accessibility training 74, 78, 106, 138, 147, 156, 157, 158

accessibility work plan 169, 173, 174

Acme Corporation 65

acquisitions 44, 46, 58, 107, 110, 131, 133, 152, 153

ADA. *See* Americans with Disabilities Act of 1990 (ADA)

advertising 83, 84, 183

aging population/workforce. *See* under disability

Americans with Disabilities Act of 1990 (ADA) 4, 5, 6, 23, 25, 76, 86, 204, 207

assessment 4, 47, 65, 88, 102, 137, 141, 142, 152, 153

assistive technology xiv, 48, 52, 120, 145, 146, 149, 182, 184, 188, 198, 199, 209

    medical or occupational health 89

    screen readers 118, 182

ATMs (automatic teller machines) 1, 201

audits 54, 88, 105, 193, 194

automated scanning 119

B

bids 57, 82, 97, 136

    accessibility documentation 78, 90, 96, 139, 140, 141, 144

    exceptions and xii, 28, 41, 57, 60, 62, 96, 102, 107, 149, 152

    responses 4, 47, 82, 128, 131, 135, 137, 138, 139, 140, 142, 143, 144, 146, 147, 148, 153

business controls 54, 64, 87, 88, 89, 103, 193

business transformation 13, 14, 221. *See also* IT accessibility transformation

business value 21, 27

C

CMS. *See* content management system

communications ix, 17, 52, 57, 80, 84, 85, 162, 185, 190, 210

    accessibility and xvii, 13, 22, 39, 53, 62, 120, 121, 123, 130, 175, 197

    coordinators and 58, 59, 61, 62, 69, 74, 75, 94, 155

    internal communications 84, 85

    marketing communications 84

competitive advantage 20, 28, 40, 78. *See also* compliance

competitive analysis 164, 191

compliance xii, xv, 2, 4, 21, 27, 28, 29, 34, 40, 46, 54, 55, 57, 60, 62, 64, 67, 68, 80, 86, 87, 88, 89, 90, 96, 97, 102, 103, 104, 105, 107, 108, 110, 113, 132, 133, 135, 145, 152, 153, 156, 172, 174, 176, 179, 189, 207, 209

    accessibility project office 51, 53, 71

    acquisitions and 107

    assessment (metrics and tracking) 190

    audit approach 105

    automated scanning 119

    bids and 97

compliance department/office 64, 87, 88

content management system 85, 118, 159, 172, 208

coordinators 58, 59, 61, 62, 69, 74, 75, 94, 155. *See* accessibility coordinators

cost and funding 67

cost-of-business exercise 31

    disability issues and 21, 184

recruitment and training ix, xii, 16, 23, 24, 30, 31, 32, 44, 57, 61, 62, 69, 74, 78, 82, 85, 86, 97, 101, 105, 106, 115, 116, 125, 130, 132, 138, 146, 147, 155, 156, 157, 158, 172, 180, 183, 184, 189, 197, 202

costs 11, 24, 31, 32, 37, 38, 67, 68, 69, 71, 73, 75, 154. *See also* accessibility program cost and funding

criteria for accessibility policy 44, 46, 97, 104

    education and training ix, 85, 116

    employees with disability and x, xi, xv, 20, 25, 30, 31, 84, 155, 162, 164, 180, 181, 184

    exceptions xii, 28, 41, 57, 60, 62, 96, 102, 107, 149

    government-purchased IT 11, 87

    internal IT x, xi, xv, 7, 25, 54, 55, 64, 79, 80, 83, 85, 86, 87, 97, 105, 110, 114, 121, 153, 155, 158, 177, 185, 189

    legal department 86

    noncompliance xii, xvii, 20, 83, 96, 189

    procurement and 221

    public-sector marketplace 27

    reporting and 104, 105, 107, 112, 157, 172

    Section 508 (Rehabilitation Act of 1973) xiii, xv, 2, 3, 4, 6, 81, 86, 130, 135, 138, 204, 207, 209

D

databases 79, 164

Department of Justice (DOJ) 4, 24, 33

Department of Labor (DOL) 19, 20, 31, 32

disability xi, 6, 7, 19, 20, 21, 24, 25, 26, 32, 81, 164, 166, 176, 180, 181, 182, 184, 197, 200, 206

    aging population/workforce xi, 29, 30

    Disability Discrimination Act of 1995 208

    Law of the People's Republic of China on the Protection of Disabled Persons 6

disability laws 7

    Americans with Disabilities Act of 1990 (ADA) 4, 5

Disability Rights Advocates 22

disabled employees. *See* employees with disabilities

disabled individuals. (*see* employees with disabilities; people with disabilities) laws on (see disability laws)

discrimination x, xi, 11, 49, 76, 180, 184

    lawsuits xii, 5, 11, 24, 25, 35

diversity x, xi, 30, 32, 79, 114, 180, 181, 193, 197

    technological diversity 114

DOJ. *See* Department of Justice

DOL. *See* Department of Labor

E

education employees with disabilities 27, 196

    accessibility and xvii, 13, 22, 39, 53, 62, 120, 121, 123, 130, 175, 197

equal access 2, 26, 35

    accessibility discrimination lawsuits 184

    demographics for 19, 20

hiring and x
productivity 10, 25, 31, 32, 48, 49, 172, 181
recent disability 5
workplace accommodations for 184
equal access for the disabled 2, 26
experts xii, xvii, 8, 29, 38, 57, 65, 78, 80, 81, 82, 114, 118, 154, 158, 169, 170, 185, 191
accessibility experts 78, 80, 82, 154, 158, 169, 170
education and training ix, xii, 16, 23, 24, 31, 32, 57, 61, 62, 74, 78, 85, 86, 97, 101, 105, 106, 115, 116, 130, 138, 146, 147, 155, 156, 157, 158, 172, 183, 189, 197, 202
manual inspection by 118
procurement and 221
subunit accessibility 59, 60, 62, 94, 114

F

Federal Register 4
Fingerhut, Barry K. 19
coordinators funding.
See accessibility program cost and funding
"The Missing Link: Financing the Industry," 19

G

guidance documentation 94, 95

H

Health and Human Services Commission 26
human resources xvii, 26, 69, 76, 82, 151, 180

human resources department 76, 180

I

IBM xiii, xiv, xv, xvi, 2, 40, 79, 196, 221
inaccessibility lawsuits.
See accessibility-related lawsuits
information technology. See all specific IT and accessibility topics
infrastructure x, 20, 27, 30, 55, 68, 72, 73, 80, 85, 94, 114, 157, 183
accessibility standards and 6, 7
funding and 53, 68
internal IT and 55, 105
lack of xii, 2, 5, 8, 22, 24, 25, 30, 68, 82, 90, 122, 138, 139, 192
websites ix, 3, 5, 7, 24, 25, 29, 33, 34, 35, 80, 83, 84, 87, 94, 95, 102, 103, 106, 114, 118, 119, 122, 125, 127, 128, 130, 142, 155
integration xiv, xvi, 13, 16, 46, 55, 60, 65, 68, 69, 73, 78, 79, 88, 97, 98, 99, 100, 101, 103, 108, 123, 130, 133, 146, 147, 153, 154, 157, 167, 179, 206, 221
accessibility integration into process. (see process integration)
internal IT x, xi, xv, 7, 25, 54, 55, 64, 79, 80, 83, 85, 86, 87, 97, 105, 110, 114, 121, 153, 155, 158, 177, 185, 189
accessibility ix, x, xi, xv, 7, 52, 53, 79, 80, 83, 85, 106, 110, 122, 155, 158

accessibility integration 99, 100, 103, 146
acquisitions 44, 46, 58, 107, 110, 131, 133, 152, 153
compliance report 135
human resources and xvii, 26, 76, 151, 180
inaccessibility 81
program placement 189
training ix, xii, 16, 23, 24, 31, 32, 57, 61, 62, 74, 78, 85, 86, 97, 101, 105, 106, 115, 116, 130, 138, 146, 147, 155, 156, 157, 158, 172, 183, 189, 197, 202
International Business Machines. See IBM
international IT accessibility standards 3
Internet 4, 10, 11, 64, 81, 96, 107, 158, 159, 161, 190, 191, 207, 209
intranet 64, 79, 85, 86, 94, 104, 107, 158, 159, 190
IT accessibility ix, x, xi, xii, xiii, xiv, xv, xvi, xvii, 2, 3, 6, 7, 13, 14, 15, 16, 19, 21, 25, 27, 30, 31, 33, 37, 38, 39, 40, 41, 42, 43, 44, 45, 47, 48, 51, 60, 61, 62, 63, 67, 71, 73, 75, 77, 78, 81, 82, 86, 87, 88, 89, 90, 93, 94, 96, 97, 98, 99, 100, 101, 102, 103, 105, 108, 109, 110, 111, 113, 114, 116, 117, 120, 121, 123, 124, 125, 126, 127, 131, 134, 135, 136, 137, 138, 139, 140, 141, 143, 144, 146, 147, 148, 149, 151, 152, 153, 154, 155, 156, 157, 158, 159, 161, 162, 164, 167, 169, 170, 171, 172, 174, 175, 176, 179, 180, 184, 187, 188, 189, 190, 191, 192, 193, 194, 206, 207, 208, 221. See also all pertinent topics
accessibility technology gap 7

compliance. See compliance
disability demographics, impact on 20
diversity perspective 30
infrastructure. (see infrastructure)
internal IT. (see internal IT)
lawsuits. (see accessibility-related lawsuits)
main areas of justification. (see business value; risk management)
procurement. (see procurement)
project integration and 101
IT accessibility policy 3, 39, 44, 51, 93, 94, 97, 102, 131, 147, 170, 221
development team/process xiv, 16, 29, 42, 68, 78, 98, 117, 138, 150, 163
exceptions xii, 28, 41, 57, 60, 62, 96, 102, 107, 149
governance of 112
technical criteria 40
IT accessibility program 39, 45, 96, 101, 153, 170, 187, 189
centralized IT accessibility 63, 71, 86, 105, 156
coordinators. (see accessibility coordinators)
funding 52, 53, 55, 67, 68, 70, 71, 72, 73, 74, 75, 77, 79, 171, 190
guidance documentation 94, 95
integration into a process. (see process integration)
management sponsorship 44, 51, 52, 53, 55, 208
metrics and tracking (assessment) 105, 190
placement 53, 54, 209

proposal for 37, 101
revenue and 34, 177
subunits 58, 59, 68, 70, 72, 73,
    74, 75, 94, 102, 103, 106
taxation of 72
visibility xii, 22, 24, 34, 190
web commerce and 80
IT accessibility transformation
    67, 93
    costs 11, 24, 31, 32, 37, 38, 67, 68,
        69, 71, 73, 75, 154
    funding 67, 70, 71, 72, 74
    manual testing 69, 74, 104,
        154, 161
IT hardware and software 69
    accessibility transformation
        costs 68, 69, 70
    internal IT x, xi, xv, 7, 25, 54, 55,
        64, 79, 80, 83, 85, 86, 87,
        97, 105, 110, 114, 121, 153,
        155, 158, 177, 185, 189
    product dev xiv, xv, 54, 55, 78,
        96, 114, 130, 147, 153,
        164, 221

J

JAN. *See* Job Accommodation
    Network
JAWS (Job Access With Speech)
    xiii, 22, 118, 138, 145
Job Accommodation Network
    (JAN) 31, 32

L

Law of the People's Republic of
    China on the Protection of
    Disabled Persons 6
laws on IT accessibility 7, 20, 25, 34
    equal access for the disabled 2,
        26, 35

Rehabilitation Act of 1973
    (Section 508) xiii, 2, 204
lawsuits. *See* accessibility-related
    lawsuits

M

managing risks. *See* risk
    management
marketing 29, 57, 64, 65, 69, 78, 80,
    83, 84, 115, 136, 176, 191
    product accessibility features
        29, 121, 176, 182
    universal design 29
    web sites and 22, 160
market intelligence 191, 192, 209
marketplace xii, xv, 21, 27, 43, 56, 79,
    102, 114, 152, 174, 190, 192, 193
    business value in 21, 27
    disability and 20
    increased share 21
    noncompliance and xii, xvii, 20,
        83, 96, 189
    product development and
        54, 96
    project plans and 88, 173
    risk management in 21
Maurer, Marc 26
"Missing Link, The: Financing the
    Industry" (Fingerhut) 19

N

National Federation of the Blind
    (NFB) 22, 23, 24, 26, 203. *See
    also* risk management

O

Office of Disability Employment
    Policy (ODEP) 31, 32, 183
Oracle Systems (Oracle
    Corporation) 26

organizational enablement 16, 169, 188, 208

P

people with disabilities ix, x, xi, xvii, 1, 2, 3, 4, 5, 6, 7, 19, 20, 22, 27, 29, 33, 119, 162, 163, 164, 165, 166, 167, 175, 176, 180, 181, 182, 183, 184, 190, 196, 207, 208, 210
  accessibility and xvii, 13, 22, 39, 53, 62, 120, 121, 123, 130, 175, 197
  accessibility lawsuits 25
  demographics for 19, 20
  hiring and x
  market and 189
  support infrastructure for 183
  usability and 162
  web commerce and 80
physical accessibility 34. *See also* IT accessibility
private sector ix, xvi, 6, 28, 69, 71, 96, 115, 134
  accessibility policies 39
  IT accessibility funding 70
  marketing support 69
  procurement xii, xiii, xvii, 5, 22, 44, 46, 47, 60, 64, 78, 79, 80, 81, 82, 83, 86, 96, 97, 100, 108, 121, 122, 123, 124, 125, 126, 127, 130, 131, 133, 134, 135, 136, 137, 139, 140, 143, 144, 146, 148, 152, 156, 157, 162, 164, 221
  stakeholders 41, 42, 61, 77, 78, 79, 80, 93, 97, 101, 103, 107, 109, 111, 112, 170, 174, 190, 192
process development 16
process integration 16, 97, 206, 221

accessibility exceptions 60, 62, 102, 152
audits 54, 88, 103, 105, 193, 194
metrics and tracking 105, 190
progress report xv, 104, 107
procurement xii, xiii, xvii, 5, 22, 44, 46, 47, 60, 64, 78, 79, 80, 81, 82, 83, 86, 96, 97, 100, 108, 121, 122, 123, 124, 125, 126, 127, 130, 131, 133, 134, 135, 136, 137, 139, 140, 143, 144, 146, 148, 152, 156, 157, 162, 164, 221
  accessibility integration and 99, 100, 146
  accessibility training and 138, 147
  exceptions and xii
  experts xii, xvii, 8, 29, 38, 57, 65, 78, 80, 81, 82, 114, 118, 154, 158, 169, 170, 185, 191
  federal regulations xii, xiii, 3
product development xiv, xv, 54, 78, 96, 130, 147, 153, 164, 221
  Raku-Raku cell phone (Fujitsu) 29
  stakeholder organizations 77, 103, 107, 112, 174, 194
product development department 78
productivity 10, 25, 31, 32, 48, 49, 172, 181
  compliance and 179
  recent disability and 25
progress report xv, 104, 107
  audience for 108
  content 3, 30, 74, 79, 80, 84, 85, 95, 96, 102, 109, 117, 118, 119, 128, 147, 156, 157, 159, 160, 161, 172, 198, 200, 206, 208, 209, 210
  frequency 109

motivational reporting 113
publication xvii, 118, 159
public relations 25, 33, 57
public sector 5, 27, 40, 71, 87, 183

R

Raku-Raku Cell Phone 29
Rehabilitation Act of 1973 xiii,
    2, 204
    Section 508 xiii, xv, 2, 3, 4, 6,
        81, 86, 130, 135, 138, 204,
        207, 209
reporting. See progress report
revenue xiv, 2, 22, 25, 28, 34, 65, 71,
    78, 84, 88, 175, 176, 177, 188,
    191, 192
    accessibility and xvii, 13, 22, 39,
        53, 62, 120, 121, 123, 130,
        175, 197
    risks and 67, 152
risk management 21
    global IT marketplace 21
    hardware and software xiii, 69,
        89, 181
    National Federation of the Blind
        lawsuits 22, 26
risks xiii, 27, 30, 67, 83, 102, 108, 152,
    154, 159, 175
    accessibility initiative and xv,
        37, 51
    accessibility-integration and
        73, 108
    acquisitions and 44, 46, 131, 133
    disabled people/employees and
        27, 30, 48, 195

S

sales 22, 28, 29, 55, 78, 84, 115, 136,
    147, 176, 191
scan tools 70, 104, 106, 119, 160,
    161, 172

screen access technology 22
screen readers 81, 118, 120, 145, 161,
    166, 167, 182, 199
    web commerce and 81
    website inaccessibility lawsuits
        xii, 81
search engine optimization 30
Section 508 (Amendment to
    Rehabilitation Act of 1973).
    See under Rehabilitation Act
    of 1973
SEO. See search engine
    optimization
Sexton, Bruce F. 22, 24
social media 84, 125
social responsibility 2, 33
software architecture ix
speech-to-text technology 29
stakeholder organizations 77,
    103, 107, 112, 174, 194. See
    also progress report
    accessibility policy
        development and 39, 40,
        42, 44, 46, 52, 56, 131, 132
    advertising and marketing 83
    compliance office 64, 87, 88
    education and learning xv, 48,
        86, 115, 194
    human resources xvii, 26, 76,
        151, 180
    internal communications 84, 85
    internal IT x, xi, xv, 7, 25, 54, 55,
        79, 80, 83, 85, 86, 87, 97,
        105, 110, 114, 121, 153, 155,
        158, 177, 189
    legal department 86
    medical or occupational
        health 89
    personnel x, xv, xvii, 10, 30, 83,
        84, 86, 88, 89, 98, 189

procurement xii, xiii, xvii, 5, 22, 44, 46, 47, 60, 64, 78, 79, 80, 81, 82, 83, 86, 96, 97, 100, 108, 121, 122, 123, 124, 125, 126, 127, 130, 131, 133, 134, 135, 136, 137, 139, 140, 143, 144, 146, 148, 152, 156, 157, 162, 164, 221

product development xiv, xv, 54, 78, 96, 114, 130, 147, 153, 164, 221

reporting and 53

web commerce and websites 3

subunit accessibility 59, 60, 62, 94, 114

    funding 52, 53, 55, 67, 68, 70, 71, 72, 73, 74, 75, 77, 79, 171, 190

T

Target Corporation 22, 23, 24

technical consulting 57, 73, 114, 116

technical enablement 7, 13, 14, 120, 155, 194, 206, 208

test tools. *See* under accessibility tools

Texas Workforce Commission 26

text-to-speech technology 2, 29, 118, 120, 207

third-parties 13, 90, 91, 97, 118, 146, 151

third-party IT accessibility 3

    certification 3, 23, 52, 145, 146, 158, 221

    third-parties 13, 86, 90, 91, 97, 118, 146, 151

tools. *See* accessibility tools training; *See* accessibility training

U

universal design 29

usability 119, 162, 163, 164, 165, 166, 167, 197, 200, 205, 208, 210, 221

usable access 166

    accessibility procurement and 125

    accessibility testing and 150, 191

    accuracy issues 60, 62, 103, 135, 144, 146

    acquisitions and 44, 46, 131, 133

    bid solicitations and 82

    competitive analysis and 191

    product development and 54, 96

    testing for 165, 197, 198, 201

    Voluntary Product Accessibility Templates (VPATs) 57, 128

    World Wide Web Consortium 3, 203, 204, 210

V

VPATs. *See* Voluntary Product Accessibility Templates

W

WAI. *See* Web Accessibility Initiative

WCAG (Web Content Accessibility Guidelines) 3, 5, 6, 117, 126, 127, 128, 130, 136, 138, 160, 172, 195, 198, 210

    Version 2.0 3, 5, 117, 126, 128, 130, 135, 156, 160, 172

Web Accessibility Initiative (WAI) 3, 203, 204

web conference 17, 18, 157

web content 3, 30, 79, 95, 128,
    206, 210
web page checkers 118, 120
websites ix, 3, 5, 7, 24, 25, 29, 33, 34,
    35, 80, 83, 84, 87, 94, 95, 102,
    103, 106, 114, 118, 119, 122, 125,
    127, 128, 130, 142, 155
    accessibility ix, x, xi, xii, xiii,
        xiv, xv, xvi, xvii, 2, 3, 5, 6,
        7, 8, 9, 11, 13, 14, 15, 16, 19,
        20, 21, 22, 23, 25, 27, 28,
        29, 30, 31, 32, 33, 34, 35,
        37, 38, 39, 40, 41, 42, 43,
        44, 45, 46, 47, 48, 49, 51,
        52, 53, 54, 55, 56, 57, 58,
        59, 60, 61, 62, 63, 64, 65,
        67, 68, 69, 70, 71, 72, 73, 74,
        75, 76, 77, 78, 79, 80, 81, 82,
        83, 84, 85, 86, 87, 88, 89,
        90, 91, 93, 94, 95, 96, 97,
        98, 99, 100, 101, 102, 103,
        104, 105, 106, 107, 108,
        109, 110, 111, 112, 113, 114,
        115, 116, 117, 118, 119, 120,
        121, 122, 123, 124, 125, 126,
        127, 128, 130, 131, 132, 133,
        134, 135, 136, 137, 138, 139,
        140, 141, 142, 143, 144, 145,
        146, 147, 148, 149, 150, 151,
        152, 153, 154, 155, 156, 157,
        158, 159, 160, 161, 162, 163,
        164, 166, 167, 169, 170, 171,
        172, 173, 174, 175, 176, 179,
        180, 181, 184, 187, 188, 189,
        190, 191, 192, 193, 194, 195,
        196, 197, 198, 200, 201,
        202, 203, 204, 205, 206,
        207, 208, 209, 210, 221
    advertising and marketing 83
    exceptions xii, 28, 41, 57, 60, 62,
        96, 102, 107, 149, 152
    external sites 86, 106, 125, 128
    inaccessibility lawsuits xii
    scan tools 70, 104, 106, 119, 160,
        161, 172
World Wide Web 3, 4, 203, 204, 210

ABOUT THE AUTHOR

Jeff Kline, is a native of Youngstown, Ohio. He is a recognized subject matter expert in keys areas of IT accessibility that include policy, rulemaking, process integration, procurement and risk mitigation. He currently serves as Program Director of Statewide Electronic and Information Resources (EIR) Accessibility at the Texas Department of Information Resources and consults on IT accessibility policy matters for federal agencies, NGOs, and accessibility certification bodies. Prior to his current position in public service, Mr. Kline managed IBM's Worldwide Accessibility Consulting and Business Transformation initiatives and held other management positions in research and product development during his 26 year IBM career including industrial design, operating system UI development, and system usability. He earned a Bachelor of Science in Industrial Design from Ohio State University and holds more than twenty patents. Mr, Kline works part-time as a professional club/lounge dj, and enjoys renovating Porsche cars, traveling, sailing, and scuba diving.

Printed in Great Britain
by Amazon

72893898R00144